Accumulism

A Philosophy of Learning

By Stanley R. Silver

Union River Research LLC
St. Paul, Minnesota

Accumulism: A Philosophy of Learning
Copyright © 2016 by Stanley R. Silver

Printed in the United States of America
First Printing, 2016
ISBN 978-0-9966543-0-2

Union River Research LLC
1583 West Race Street
St. Paul, MN 55102

www.accumulism.com
publisher@accumulism.com

Cover Picture - The School of Athens (1511, fresco)
Raffaello Sanzio *(1483-1520) Italian painter, architect.*

Preface

This is a philosophy book. It presents a philosophy of learning, or, more accurately, a philosophy of subjective learning, which I call accumulism.

Of particular interest, this philosophy can be used to improve itself.

This book also presents a new writing form called a hectosophy, which supports and enables accumulism.

Accumulism neither solves nor explains. Rather it is a quiver of arrows; a chest of tools; a collection of ideas that can be used (or not) to learn a bit faster.

Each idea presented in this book is an opinion. Although I explain the reasoning behind some opinions, none are backed by logic or proof. The only support the opinions in this book have is that one person believes them.

I thank patient family and friends for bearing with me, as I tried and discarded learning idea after learning idea during these past many years.

I dedicate this book to my late father, Dr. Randall H. Silver, a wise man and life-long learner.

The Chapters

Introduction

As an engineer and software developer, I enjoy solving problems. In 1995, I became curious. What would happen if I made an honest effort to solve an impossible engineering problem?

I set the impossible goal of speeding up software development by a factor of ten.

Speeding up software development is a fascinating research goal, because software development is more art than it is science or engineering.

By this statement, I mean that decisions made by scientists and engineers are supported by formal analysis that shows the decisions are correct. Conversely, most decisions made by software developers are based on experience, and cannot be proven correct by formal analysis.

Not knowing how else to improve an experienced-based endeavor, I started collecting software development ideas in a journal. This helped, and I became interested in "collecting ideas" as a way to learn.

I started collecting ideas about "collecting ideas" in my journal.

The essay, novel, newspaper article, and scientific-journal article are common writing forms. In 1996, I encountered a new writing form: the pattern. A pattern is a one or two page description, with a unique name, of a good subjective solution to a common problem. A pattern language is a collection of patterns.

The pattern writing form was developed in the 1970s by Austrian-born American architect and author Christopher Alexander (1936-) to record and communicate good solutions to common architectural problems.

American software developer and inventor Ward Cunningham (1949-) adopted this writing form to record and communicate good solutions to common software development problems.

The pattern writing form is designed to communicate good subjective ideas. It is not designed to systematically improve subjective ideas.

In 1999, I was surprised to discover that making two modifications to the pattern writing form produced a writing form that *could* be used to systematically improve subjective ideas.

The first, and most important, modification was to fix the number of collected patterns to be always one hundred. The second modification was to relax the pattern so it became only a named paragraph, instead of a named solution to a common problem.

I called this new writing form a *hectosophy*, from the Greek words *hecto*, meaning one hundred, and *sophy*, meaning knowledge or wisdom. A hectosophy comprises one hundred named paragraphs.

Between 1999 and 2009, I successfully used hectosophies to improve my understanding of software development, learning, economics, and religion.

I also tried using this writing form to improve my people skills and personal efficiency, but I failed. I not only failed; I made negative progress.

At this point I had a writing form that increased personal understanding but harmed self-improvement. I was frustrated, but I was also intrigued.

Between 2009 and 2016, in an attempt to make the hectosophy writing form useful for self-improvement, I struggled to develop a deeper understanding of learning and improvement.

I started to recognize what appeared to be a type of philosophy – a philosophy of subjective learning. I present my version of this philosophy in this book, in the hopes of getting feedback to make it better.

I call my collection of insights "accumulism", from the English word *accumulate*, derived from Latin *accumulare*, meaning to amass or accumulate. The name denotes a gradual accumulation of ideas.

The first three chapters of this book are examples of hectosophies and decasophies produced using accumulism. The remaining chapters describe the development of accumulism.

Prologue

The Road to Wisdom

Trouville – A Lesson with the Rudder
(late 1800s, oil on canvas)
Paul Jobert (1863-1942), French painter.
(Trouville-sur-Mer is a town in Normandy, France)

Wisdom, compassion, and courage are the three universally recognized moral qualities of men.
Confucius (551-479 BC), Chinese philosopher.

Plato is dear to me, but dearer still is truth.
Aristotle (attributed to) (384-322 BC), Greek philosopher.

A wise man will hear, and will increase learning; and a man of understanding shall attain unto wise counsels.
Proverbs 1:5, King James Bible.

These times are the ancient times, when the world is ancient, and not those which we account ancient *ordine retrogrado,* by a computation backward from ourselves.
Francis Bacon (1561-1626), English renaissance author, statesman, philosopher.

If I have seen further… it is by standing upon the shoulders of giants.
Isaac Newton (1642-1727), English physicist, mathematician.

The aim of an argument or discussion should not be victory, but progress.
Joseph Joubert (1754-1824), French moralist and essayist.

If I have a thousand ideas and only one turns out to be good, I am satisfied.
Alfred Nobel (1822-1896), Swedish inventor of dynamite.

Truth in our ideas means their power to work.
William James (1842-1910), American philosopher.

There are some things which cannot be learned quickly, and time, which is all we have, must be paid heavily for their acquiring. They are the very simplest things and because it takes a man's life to know them the little new

that each man gets from life is very costly and the only heritage he has to leave.
Ernest Hemingway *(1899-1961), American author.*

The way to get good ideas is to get lots of ideas, and throw the bad ones away.
Linus Pauling *(1901-1994), American chemist and biologist.*

The road to wisdom?
Well, it's plain and simple to express:
Err and err and err again
But less and less and less.
Piet Hein *(1905-1996), Danish inventor, poet.*

All models are wrong, but some are useful.
George E. P. Box *(1919-2013), British born American statistician.*

Chapter I

Collecting Seashells

A Learning Hectosophy

Shiohigari (Gathering Shells)
(1810s, color woodblock print)
Utagawa, Kunitora *(1789?-1868) Japanese artist.*

Pearls of wisdom

This chapter contains a collection of ninety learning "pearls of wisdom", gathered over the course of many years. It has no theme or narration. Ideas are presented a la carte, rather than table d'hote.

Collecting seashells

Three seashell collectors spent the summer at a beach.

The first collector carried a basket that held ten shells. Each day she collected ten pretty shells in her basket. She took them home and displayed them. At the end of the summer she had hundreds of pretty shells.

The second collector carried a basket that held ten shells. He spent two weeks collecting ten very pretty shells in his basket. He took them home and displayed them. He spent the rest of the summer fishing. At the end of the summer he had ten very pretty shells.

The third collector carried a basket that held ten shells. Each day she collected ten pretty shells in her basket. She took them home. Of her existing and new shells, she kept the ten prettiest, and displayed them. At the end of the summer she had ten gorgeous shells.

Some secrets

The disciple trudged across the remote Tibetan valley and slowly pulled himself up the steep cliff. He caught his breath, knocked on the monastery door, and asked the wizened monk who answered: "Master, may I ask you a question?" The monk slowly nodded.

"What is 'the secret' of wisdom?" the disciple asked. The monk smiled and replied, "One secret of wisdom is to think plural, not singular."

The disciple smiled. "Well, then. What are 'the secrets' of wisdom?" The monk smiled and replied, "One secret of wisdom is to think partial, not final."

The disciple smiled. "Well, then. What are 'some secrets' of wisdom?" The monk smiled. The disciple smiled. "Thank you," the disciple said.

The genie of skills

A young woman saw a lamp washed up on the beach. She polished it. The face of a genie appeared in the air before her.

"I am the Genie of Skills," the genie said. "I was trapped in this lamp by my enemies. If you follow my instructions and let me out, I will grant you expertise in one skill."

The young woman said to the genie "Please let me think a minute".

She pictured herself as an expert figure skater, an expert actress, an expert businesswoman, an expert mother, an expert lawyer, an expert teacher, and an expert politician.

She then replied to the genie "Yes, I will let you out, if, in return, you grant me expertise in the skill of acquiring expertise".

Long division contest

The math contest judge looked sternly down at the girl. "What is 70 divided by ten?" asked the judge. "Seven," replied the girl. "What is 71 divided by ten?" asked the judge. "Seven point one," replied the girl.

"Hmmm," intoned the judge, concentrating, "What is an iron bar divided by ten?". "Ten iron pieces," replied the girl. "What is an iron smelting process divided by ten?" asked the judge. "Ten iron process steps," replied the girl.

"And what is the skill of blacksmithing divided by ten?" the judge asked smugly. The girl pondered for a moment. "Ten iron skillets?" she ventured. She won the contest.

Record what worked

To learn and improve, record what worked. In notebooks, on scraps of paper, or in computer documents.

Occasionally summarize

Occasionally summarize what worked into a decasophy or a hectosophy. Over time, this forces an increase in quality, not quantity.

Decasophies and Hectosophies

For convenience, the following words are defined:

decasophy (de kas' ə fee)
noun: A collection of ten subjective ideas, observations, practices, rules, or techniques. *From the Greek "deca" meaning ten, and "sophy" meaning knowledge or wisdom.*

hectosophy (hek tos' ə fee)
noun: A collection of one hundred subjective ideas, observations, practices, rules, or techniques. Sometimes composed of ten decasophies. *From the Greek "hecto" meaning one hundred, and "sophy" meaning knowledge or wisdom.*

Prithee a pithy appellation

Label ideas, observations, and practices with short, meaningful names.

Third grade student, fourth grade problem

A third grade student encountered a fourth grade problem. He pondered whether he should work hard trying to solve the problem using his third grade techniques, or put the problem aside, work hard at school, and tackle the problem when he reached the fourth grade, using fourth grade techniques.

The quickest route

Two men, each with an old car that could travel no faster than forty miles per hour, decided to drive to California from the East Coast. They would depart in one week.

The first man spent the week figuring out the shortest route to take. The second man spent the week fixing his car so it would travel faster than forty miles per hour.

Rise above it

You can't solve a problem on the same level that it was created. You have to rise above it to the next level. *Albert Einstein (1879-1955), German-born American physicist.*

Know-like-do-learn-know

If you know how to do something, you like it. If you like something, you do it. If you do something, you learn it. If you learn something, you know more about it.

This learning cycle is a positive feedback loop that has two states: *on* and *off*. You are either doing and learning, or not doing and not learning.

Learn by doing

For the things we have to learn before we can do them, we learn by doing them.
Aristotle (384-322 BC), Greek philosopher.

Machine gun approach

How do we start to learn? Or restart to learn? One way is to try anything and everything. Try one hundred small doable tasks, each vaguely related to what you want to learn.

One hundred near-random efforts will teach something. Use this knowledge to plan the next one hundred (hopefully less random) doable tasks. Eventually you will learn enough to progress in a systematic way. In other words: flail, ratchet, repeat.

The Scylla and Charybdis of learning

If you avoid the Scylla of not knowing how to learn, be wary of the Charybdis of knowing how to learn, having it be wrong, *and not changing it.*

You learn what you practice

If you practice swimming, you learn to swim. If you practice learning, you learn to learn. If you practice succeeding, you learn to succeed.

The way to succeed

The way to succeed is to double your failure rate.
Thomas J. Watson Sr. (1874-1956), American businessman, founder of IBM.

Failing to learn; learning to fail

To learn, you must conduct trial and error. Trial and error involves failure.

Since you learn what you practice, you face the very real danger of learning to fail as you attempt to learn something hard. As you try and try again to reach a difficult goal without success, your attempts become similar and halfhearted. You stop trying new things. You assume continual failure, and achieve continual failure.

Each day differently

Following rules written on paper slows trial and error, and thus learning. Do important things differently each day.

Wheel-spinner goal

A wheel-spinner goal is a goal that puts you into a try and fail loop, without making progress. Picture a car that is stuck. The accelerator is repeatedly pressed. The car does not move. Instead, it digs itself deeper into a rut.

Pot-of-gold goal (aka byproduct goal)

Like the pot of gold at the end of the rainbow, there are some goals with built-in dynamics that make them wheel-spinner goals if they are pursued directly. Progress toward such goals is best made obliquely as a byproduct of pursuing other goals.

A wild animal will not eat out of your hand if you keep walking toward it. Maximizing a company's profits in the short term cannibalizes long-term value. Pleasing everybody cannibalizes long-term success and respect.

A wild animal must come to you. Profits come from satisfying customers. If you are honest, helpful, and successful, many people will like you.

Deciduous goal

A deciduous (baby-tooth) goal is a goal set by a beginning learner that is later discarded in favor of a better learning goal.

Wittgenstein's ladder

My propositions are elucidatory in this way: he who understands me finally recognizes them as senseless, when he has climbed out through them, on them, over them. (He must so to speak throw away the ladder, after he has climbed up on it.)
Ludwig Wittgenstein (1889-1951), Austrian philosopher.

It feels like one big secret

Expertise-based endeavors, such as software development, business, and getting along with others, are improved by learning many small insights.

However, when one does not know how to do such an endeavor, it feels as if one is missing one big secret, not many small insights.

In the process of learning these many small insights, one of them may cause an "ah-ha" or a "eureka". This small "breakthrough" insight feels like one big secret.

And when one eventually becomes good at something, and tries to explain it to others, it feels as if there is one big secret to explain, not many small insights.

These feelings are real. They are as strong in good learners as in beginning learners. Good learners, however, ignore these feelings better.

Faith in God.
Faith in me.
Faith in the little rules
I can't yet see.

Bad goal or bad me

Our to-do goals involve tasks with which we are familiar.
Our learning goals, by definition, involve tasks we are less
familiar with. If our progress toward a learning goal stalls,
who or what is at fault?

Are we not smart enough? Are we not working hard
enough? Or did we choose a poor goal?

It is the goal's fault

You *are* smart enough. You *are* working hard enough. It
is the learning goal's fault.

Artificial experience

Speeding up learning often means speeding up the
acquisition of experience. Three types of goals help.

- An *emotional goal* inspires and motivates.
- A *SALI (single axis of learning and improvement)*
  defines a component of a skill. Each SALI has a
  single clear definition of better.
- A short-term *practice goal* is designed to artificially
  maximize experience. A single practice goal can
  address a single SALI or multiple SALI's.

To be state basketball champions might be an inspiring
goal for high school basketball players. Dribbling a
basketball, shooting, defense, and running plays might be
SALI's. A practice goal might be to play "follow the

leader", and have basketball players follow a leader while dribbling basketballs.

Aim at Boston, measure from yesterday.

In mathematics, a vector is defined by a direction and a magnitude. Goals also comprise a direction and a magnitude.

When pursuing a difficult goal, it is often better to measure daily progress, or progress from the starting point, than to measure remaining distance. For example, if you set a goal of walking from San Francisco to Boston, use Boston to set direction, while measuring miles walked per day, or miles walked from San Francisco.

A doable equation

undoable = $\sum$ doable

As a compass needle

Aim at perfection as a compass needle aims at north.

Perfection is the
Long-term aim,
Completion is the
Short-term game.

You, too, can become great

Keep away from people who try to belittle your ambitions. Small people always do that, but the really great make you feel that you, too, can become great.
Mark Twain (1835-1910), American writer, humorist.

Be discouraged

"Don't be discouraged" is a hard rule to follow. Be discouraged. Wallow. For a while. Then become excited again.

Scientia potentia est

Knowledge is power.
(attributed to) **Francis Bacon** *(1561-1626), English renaissance author, statesman, philosopher.*

Grace

Knowledge is but folly unless it is guided by grace.
George Herbert, *(1593-1633), Welsh-born English poet, orator, priest.*

Courage

I learned that courage was not the absence of fear, but the triumph over it.
Nelson Mandela *(1900-2013), South African politician.*

Our deepest fear

Our deepest fear is not that we are inadequate.
Our deepest fear is that we are powerful beyond measure.
It is our light, not our darkness, that most frightens us.

We ask ourselves, who am I to be brilliant,
gorgeous, talented, fabulous?
Actually, who are you not to be?

You are a child of God.
Your playing small does not serve the world.
There is nothing enlightened about shrinking
so that other people won't feel insecure around you.

We are all meant to shine, as children do.
We were born to make manifest
the glory of God that is within us.
It's not just in some of us; it is in everyone.

And as we let our own light shine,
we unconsciously give other people
permission to do the same.
As we are liberated from our own fear,
our presence automatically liberates others.
Marianne Williamson (1952-), American author.

We should all be thankful

In everyone's life, at some time, our inner fire goes out. It is then burst into flame by an encounter with another human being. We should all be thankful for those people who rekindle the inner spirit.
Albert Schweitzer (1875-1965), Alsatian theologian.

Do it anyway

People are often unreasonable, irrational, and self-centered.
Forgive them anyway.
If you are kind, people may accuse you of selfish, ulterior motives.
Be kind anyway.
If you are successful, you will win some unfaithful friends and some genuine enemies.
Succeed anyway.
If you are honest and sincere people may deceive you.
Be honest and sincere anyway.
What you spend years creating, others could destroy overnight.
Create anyway.
If you find serenity and happiness, some may be jealous.
Be happy anyway.
The good you do today, will often be forgotten.

Do good anyway.
Give the best you have, and it will never be enough.
Give your best anyway.
In the final analysis, it is between you and God.
It was never between you and them anyway.
Mother Teresa *(1910-1997), Roman Catholic nun.*
Adapted from 'The Paradoxical Commandments' by **Kent M. Keith** *(1949-) American author.*

Twenty-five years after Darwin

The known is finite, the unknown infinite; intellectually we stand on an islet in the midst of an illimitable ocean of inexplicability. Our business in every generation is to reclaim a little more land, to add something to the extent and the solidity of our possessions. And even a cursory glance at the history of the biological sciences during the last quarter of a century is sufficient to justify the assertion, that the most potent instrument for the extension of the realm of natural knowledge which has come into men's hands, since the publication of Newton's 'Principia,' is Darwin's 'Origin of Species.'

It was badly received by the generation to which it was first addressed, and the outpouring of angry nonsense to which it gave rise is sad to think upon. But the present generation will probably behave just as badly if another Darwin should arise, and inflict upon them that which the generality of mankind most hate – the necessity of revising their convictions.
Thomas Henry Huxley *(1825-1895), British biologist.*

Given with love

Whenever you have truth it must be given with love, or the message and the messenger will be rejected.
Mahatma Gandhi *(1869-1948), Indian political and spiritual leader.*

Don't shoot the message

Don't shoot the message because of the messenger.

Put the map at the back

The king gave the famous explorer a partially completed map showing the known territory of his kingdom and asked him to explore the unknown territory.

While traveling through the known territory, the explorer put the map at the head of his column, and used it to navigate.

When he began to explore the unknown territory, he put the map at the back of his column, and used it to record where he had been.

Granny gear

The long-distance bicyclist pedaled at a constant pace. When he got to a hill, he down-shifted. His bike went slower, but not his pedaling. When he got to a steep hill, he down-shifted to his lowest gear, called "granny gear". And when even that gear was not low enough, he took a different route, still pedaling at his constant pace.

AAA

In addition to reducing a list to ten or one hundred items, another culling technique is to reduce a list until all items are of equal (high) value. In other words, keep the A's, and remove the B's and C's and D's. This approach is useful for culling material things, such as clothes in a closet or boxes in an attic.

A learner of distinction

Before the young man attended butcher school, meat was meat. As he became more adept at slicing meat, meat became beef, pork, chicken, and lamb. Beef became chuck, rib, short loin, sirloin, shank, brisket, plate, and flank. Short loin became top loin steak, T-bone steak, Porterhouse steak, tenderloin roast, and tenderloin steak. And each cut of beef came in prime, choice, and select quality grades.

One for all and all for one

In complex systems, each problem is partially addressed by many practices that work. And each practice that works partially addresses many problems. In other words, there is a many-to-many relationship between problems and practices.

This makes it hard to progress by fixing one problem at a time. Instead, focus on making improvements. As you gradually improve, you gradually chip away at all problems.

Happy families

Happy families are all alike; every unhappy family is unhappy in its own way.
Leo Tolstoy (1828-1910), Russian author and philosopher.

Fixing and solving
are problematic.
Better is better.

For or against

Strive *for*, rather than *against*.

The shift

The shift from fixing problems to steady improvement is a gradual one.

Aristotle's ideas about people

The young history student read an essay on Aristotle that stated Aristotle's ideas about physics had long been superseded, but his ideas about people were as relevant today as they were 2500 years ago. At first, she smiled in agreement – after all, people had not changed in 2500 years.

But on deeper reflection, she was puzzled. Just as people had not changed in 2500 years, neither had the laws of nature.

Snowballs

Record what worked for recording what worked.
Learn the skill of learning skills.
Develop the habit of developing good habits.
Learn from others how to learn from others.

Love to learn
To love to learn

Beware the urge

When recording what worked:

> Beware the urge for correctness.
> Beware the urge for completeness.
> Beware the urge for consistency.
> Watch out for the desire to fit things into patterns.

A collection of what worked is messy, incomplete, and contradictory.

Very well then

Do I contradict myself? Very well then I contradict myself.
I am large, I contain multitudes.
Walt Whitman (1819-1892), American poet.

Simple Pragmatism and Pure Elegance

Simple Pragmatism is the plain and hard-working little
sister of the beautiful and alluring Pure Elegance. If you
marry Simple Pragmatism, be careful. Since Simple
Pragmatism and Pure Elegance are related, Pure Elegance
will be seductively near. It is OK to admire her, and even
desire her, but you must never embrace her. If Simple
Pragmatism catches you in the arms of Pure Elegance, she
will divorce you.

Single ideas

Beware the urge to analyze single subjective ideas. All
subjective ideas have flaws and merits, and are better
analyzed by comparing them to other subjective ideas.

Improvement tax

During each time interval or task, use some percentage of
time for improvement. Improve your environment, tools,
and techniques. Record what worked.

Riding a half-tamed horse

Sometimes it seems we are five percent rational beings and
ninety-five percent habitual beings. As if we are in charge
of ourselves the same way a rider is in charge of a half-
tamed horse.

Remaking ourselves

As human beings, our greatness lies not so much in being able to remake the world – that is the myth of the atomic age – as in being able to remake ourselves.
Mahatma Gandhi (1869-1948), Indian political and spiritual leader.

Braver

I count him braver who overcomes his desires than him who overcomes his enemies.
Aristotle (384-322 BC), Greek philosopher.

What we are capable of doing

The difference between what we do and what we are capable of doing would suffice to solve most of the world's problems.
Mahatma Gandhi (1869-1948), Indian political and spiritual leader.

Excellence

If you want to achieve excellence, you can get there today. As of this second, quit doing less-than-excellent work.
Thomas J. Watson Sr. (1874-1956), American businessman, founder of IBM.

Acquire quality

Men acquire a particular quality by constantly acting a particular way...you become just by performing just actions, temperate by performing temperate actions, brave by performing brave actions.
Aristotle (384-322 BC), Greek philosopher.

Agreeable

Choose the life that is most useful, and habit will make it the most agreeable.
Francis Bacon *(1561-1626), English renaissance author, statesman, philosopher.*

Francis Bacon

Bacon left a heritage to English science. His writings and his thoughts are not always clear, but he firmly held, and, with the authority which his personal eminence gave him, firmly proclaimed, that the careful and systematic investigation of natural phenomena and their accurate record would give to man a power in this world which, in his time, was hardly to be conceived.

He did more than anyone else to help to free the intellect from preconceived notions and to direct it to the unbiased study of facts, whether of nature, of mind, or of society; he vindicated an independent position for the positive sciences; and to this, in the main, he owes his position in the history of modern thought.

Though Bacon did not make any one single advance in natural knowledge – though his precepts, as Whewell reminds us, "are now practically useless" – yet he used his great talents, his high position, to enforce upon the world a new method of wrenching from nature her secrets and, with tireless patience and untiring passion, impressed upon his contemporaries the conviction that there was "a new unexplored Kingdom of Knowledge within the reach and grasp of man, if he will be humble enough, and patient enough, and truthful enough to occupy it."

The Cambridge history of English and American literature, *ed. by A.W. Ward et al., New York: G.P. Putnam's Sons; Cambridge: University Press, 1907-21*

The idea of progress

Though it is hard to pinpoint the birth of an idea, for all intents and purposes the modern idea of technological "progress" (in the sense of a steady, cumulative, historical advance in applied scientific knowledge) began with Bacon's *The Advancement of Learning* and became fully articulated in his later works.

That history might in fact be progressive, i.e., an onward and upward ascent – and not, as Aristotle had taught, merely cyclical or, as cultural pessimists from Hesiod to Spengler have supposed, a descending or retrograde movement – became for Bacon an article of secular faith which he propounded with evangelical force and a sense of mission. In the Advancement, the idea is offered tentatively, as a kind of hopeful hypothesis. But in later works such as the New Organon, it becomes almost a promised destiny: Enlightenment and a better world, Bacon insists, lie within our power; they require only the cooperation of learned citizens and the active development of the arts and sciences.

The Internet Encyclopedia of Philosophy
http://www.iep.utm.edu/b/bacon.htm (03/26/2014).

Sharing subjective theories

Influenced by the amazing power of the scientific method coupled with peer-reviewed journals, we often attempt to share subjective ideas the same way we share natural-science ideas: as single theories, supported by rational arguments.

Single theories and reproducible experiments are the bricks of which science is built. Unfortunately, single theories seem of less value when sharing subjective ideas.

Without the backing of repeatable experiments, people quibble over them. Even worse than complete rejection, single subjective theories lead to partial agreement. If one author agrees with eighty percent of another author's theory, she must propose a new theory to express her viewpoint. The result is two competing theories with a small difference.

Is there a better format?

Is there a better format than single theories for sharing subjective ideas? A format that better allows us to disagree with, learn from, and add to each other's views?

Comparing boxes of apples and boxes of apples

The judge walked among the apple stands at the county fair. One stand displayed three big apples. Another displayed a basket of apples decorated with flowers. Yet another stand displayed a pyramid of fifty-five apples.

"How can I fairly compare these displays?" the judge asked himself.

He had an idea. He gave each stand an identical box that held ten apples. "Put your ten best apples in this box," he said, "and I will select the stand with the best box".

Combining boxes of apples

The state fair was one week later. Instead of entering the box of apples that had won first prize at the county fair, the apple stand owners decided to combine their boxes. They created a new box, with the ten best apples from the existing boxes, and entered the new box at the state fair.

Forward thinking

The following paragraph is a part of the forward written by **Ward Cunningham** (1949-), an American software developer and the inventor of wiki web sites, for the book *The Pragmatic Programmer*, by Andrew Hunt and David Thomas:

…The authors have been careful to avoid proposing a theory of software development. This is fortunate, because if they had they would be obliged to warp each chapter to defend their theory. … I've studied this problem for a dozen years and found the most promise in a device called a pattern language.

Theory

Theory is a friend of science, and a subtle enemy of philosophy.

Consensus

Consensus is a friend of joint action, and a subtle enemy of joint learning.

Observation

Observation is a friend of everybody.

Subjective group research – to each his own

Hectosophies signed by multiple authors are not useful. When Tommy's group researches a subjective topic, each person in the group produces his or her own hectosophy.

Subjective group action – consensus is needed

Groups designed for action need rules and processes. When Tina's group works on a project, they jointly agree on rules and processes to follow during the project.

For my software developer friends

The learning approaches explored in this book hint at the following two new software development approaches.

1. Do not formalize a single company-wide set of software development practices. Rather, define and strictly follow a new set of software development practices for each software project. Record what worked after each project.

2. Have two backlogs. Work on the customer backlog (prioritized by the customer) eighty percent of the time. Work on the team backlog (prioritized by the team lead) twenty percent of the time.

A liberal arts education

I received an engineering college education. My education comprised teaching and training. I was taught to solve engineering problems, and trained to solve engineering problems.

I solved thousands of example engineering problems by the time I graduated.

After talking to many people with liberal arts college educations, two benefits of such an education intrigue me. One benefit is an increased humanities vocabulary, which allows a more detailed mental model of, and therefore a better understanding of, human nature.

A second, perhaps more important, benefit is years of training in subjective decision making, through paper writing and class discussion.

Read and choose, and talk and choose, and read and choose, and talk and choose, over and over and over.

A vision

A vision... Experts are convened in a room, discussing a subjective topic. Each presents ten ideas that work for him or her. There are questions, but no debate.

The experts adjourn to modify their presentations, based on what they learned from each other. They reconvene to each present their revised sets of ten ideas, then socialize and go home, each a little wiser.

L' Envoi

When Earth's last picture is painted and the tubes are twisted and dried,
When the oldest colours have faded, and the youngest critic has died,
We shall rest, and, faith, we shall need it -- lie down for an aeon or two,
Till the Master of All Good Workmen shall put us to work anew!

And those that were good shall be happy: they shall sit in a golden chair;
They shall splash at a ten-league canvas with brushes of comets' hair;
They shall find real saints to draw from -- Magdalene, Peter, and Paul;
They shall work for an age at a sitting and never be tired at all!

And only the Master shall praise us, and only the Master shall blame;
And no one shall work for money, and no one shall work for fame,
But each for the joy of the working, and each, in his separate star,

Shall draw the Thing as he sees It for the God of things as they are!
Rudyard Kipling *(1865-1936), British author, poet.*

A dark and stormy night

It was a dark and stormy night. Fred Ranck (Ph.D., mathematics) walked briskly out of the set theory conference in the "Mediterranean" room of the big uptown hotel, and hurried down the corridor, clutching his PowerPoint slides and Mountain Dew cola. Susan Tyne (Ph.D., philosophy) wandered slowly out of the history of philosophy seminar in the "Aegean" room of the same hotel, balancing 84 index-carded notes on how Darwin's theory of evolution affected philosophy, and one Starbucks coffee.

She paused at the corner, her eyes absently noting the wave-like patterns of the corridor lights on the long expanse of blue-green carpet, deep in thought about philosophy and evolution. He barreled around the corner. Lighting flashed, thunder bashed. Researchers crashed, coffee and cola splashed. Slides and cards were mashed in a heap on the floor.

"You got philosophy and coffee on my set theory!" yelped the mathematician.

"You got set theory and cola in my philosophy!" exclaimed the philosopher.

They looked down. The pile wriggled and writhed. Suddenly what looked like a brown and yellow origami centipede slithered from under the papers.

"Wh-What are you?" gulped Dr. Fred Ranck.

"I am a sophy-set," said the creature, matter-of-factly.

"Wh-What do you want?" stammered Dr. Susan Tyne.

"I want to find a sophy-set of the opposite gender," chuckled the sophy-set.

"Wh-Why?" mumbled Drs. F. Ranck and S. Tyne together.

"Why do you think?" chortled the sophy-set. "I want to make baby sophy-sets."

The humanities, of course

A humanities course is designed to expose students to a subjective topic. It presents to students many opinions, then requires them to form and articulate their own opinion by writing papers and discoursing in class.

A humanities course that taught learning might be a powerful course. Learning opinions and case studies could be presented to students, who would be required to form their own opinion of learning by discoursing in class and recording what worked for them.

Improving improvement

Learning to speak accelerated human improvement. Writing accelerated human improvement. Printing accelerated human improvement. The invention of Western science accelerated human improvement. The development of formal process improvement and quality improvement in the mid-1900s accelerated human improvement.

The following Wikipedia articles about quality improvement are of interest.

Training Within Industry

http://en.wikipedia.org/wiki/Training_Within_Industry (03/26/2014).

The Training Within Industry (TWI) service was created by the United States Department of War, running from 1940 to 1945 within the War Manpower Commission. The purpose was to provide consulting services to war-related industries whose personnel were being conscripted into the US Army at the same time the War Department was issuing orders for additional materiel. It was apparent that the shortage of trained and skilled personnel at precisely the time they were needed most would impose a hardship on those industries, and that only improved methods of job training would address the shortfall. By the end of World War II, over 1.6 million workers in over 16,500 plants had received a certification.

Although the TWI program was abandoned at the end of the war, the instruction methods were introduced to the war-torn nations of Europe and Asia... It was especially well-received in Japan, where TWI formed the basis of the kaizen culture in industry. Kaizen, known by such names as Quality Circles in the West, was successfully harnessed by Toyota Motor Corporation in conjunction with the Lean or Just In Time principles of Taiichi Ohno. In the Forward to Dinero's book "Training Within Industry" (2005), John Shook relates a story in which a Toyota trainer brought out an old copy of a TWI service manual to prove to him that American workers at NUMMI could be taught using the "Japanese" methods used at Toyota. Thus, TWI was the forerunner of what is today regarded as a Japanese creation.

Walter A. Shewhart

http://en.wikipedia.org/wiki/Shewhart (03/26/2014).

Walter Andrew Shewhart (1891-1967) was an American physicist, engineer and statistician, sometimes known as the father of statistical quality control.

When Dr. Shewhart joined the Western Electric Company Inspection Engineering Department at the Hawthorne Works in 1918, industrial quality was limited to inspecting finished products and removing defective items. That all changed on May 16, 1924. Dr. Shewhart's boss, George D. Edwards, recalled: "Dr. Shewhart prepared a little memorandum only about a page in length. About a third of that page was given over to a simple diagram which we would all recognize today as a schematic control chart. That diagram, and the short text which preceded and followed it, set forth all of the essential principles and considerations which are involved in what we know today as process quality control."

In 1938 his work came to the attention of physicists W. Edwards Deming and Raymond T. Birge... The encounter began a long collaboration between Shewhart and Deming that involved work on productivity during World War II and Deming's championing of Shewhart's ideas in Japan from 1950 onwards. Deming developed some of Shewhart's methodological proposals around scientific inference and named his synthesis the Shewhart cycle.

W. Edwards Deming

http://en.wikipedia.org/wiki/Edward_Deming (03/26/2014).

William Edwards Deming (October 14, 1900-December 20, 1993) was an American statistician, college professor, author, lecturer, and consultant...

In 1947, Deming was involved in early planning for the 1951 Japanese Census. The Allied powers were occupying Japan, and he was asked by the United States Department of the Army to assist with the census. He was brought over at the behest of General Douglas MacArthur, who grew frustrated at being unable to complete so much as a phone call without the line going dead due to Japans shattered post-war economy. While in Japan, his expertise in quality control techniques, combined with his involvement in Japanese society, brought him an invitation from the Japanese Union of Scientists and Engineers (JUSE).

JUSE members had studied Shewhart's techniques, and as part of Japan's reconstruction efforts, they sought an expert to teach statistical control. From June–August 1950, Deming trained hundreds of engineers, managers, and scholars in statistical process control (SPC) and concepts of quality. He also conducted at least one session for top management (including top Japanese industrialists of the likes of Akio Morita, the cofounder of Sony Corp.) Deming's message to Japan's chief executives was that improving quality would reduce expenses while increasing productivity and market share. Perhaps the best known of these management lectures was delivered at the Mt. Hakone Conference Center in August 1950.

A number of Japanese manufacturers applied his techniques widely and experienced heretofore unheard-of levels of quality and productivity. The improved quality combined with the lowered cost created new international demand for Japanese products.

Plan–Do–Check–Act Cycle

http://en.wikipedia.org/wiki/PDCA (03/26/2014).

PDCA (plan–do–check–act or plan–do–check–adjust) is an iterative four-step management method used in business for the control and continuous improvement of processes and products. It is also known as the Deming circle/cycle/wheel, Shewhart cycle, control circle/cycle, or plan–do–study–act (PDSA)... PDCA was made popular by Dr W. Edwards Deming, who is considered by many to be the father of modern quality control; however, he always referred to it as the "Shewhart cycle". Later in Deming's career, he modified PDCA to "Plan, Do, Study, Act" (PDSA) because he felt that "check" emphasized inspection over analysis.

Chapter II

Team Worth

An Economic Decasophy

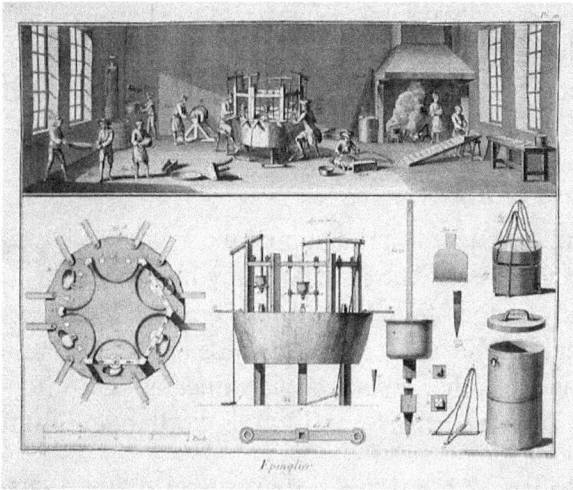

Epinglier, Plate III (Pin Making) (1762, engraving)
An illustration in Encyclopédie, edited by
Denis Diderot *(1713-1784), French philosopher.*
Artist: **Louis-Jacques Goussier** *(1722-1799), French illustrator.*
Engraver: **Benoit Louis Prevost** *(1735-1804), French engraver.*

Economic opinions

This chapter presents personal economic opinions, slowly collected and expanded over a period of several years.

A riddle

Kerry and Peggy have $100,000 in the bank. They decide to build a house. They pay $100,000 to an architect, contractor, and workers to construct the house. They end up with a $100,000 house, and, after expenses, the architect, contractor, and workers end up with $50,000 in the bank. Where did the extra $50,000 come from?

Another riddle

Four entrepreneurs start a company. Investors have $1 million to invest. The investors buy half the new company's stock for $1 million, and the founders keep the other half of the stock. The business has $1 million in the bank, and no other assets, but is valued at $2 million. Where does the extra $1 million of worth come from?

The worth of work hours and business hours

The $50,000 of new worth in Kerry and Peggy's house seems to have been extracted from the work hours put in by the architect, contractor, and workers.

The $1 million of worth created by the business seems to represent the worth of future profits of the business. Since profits come from the operation of the company, the extra $1 million can be said to represent the worth of future business hours.

A definition of worth

It seems that hours of work, or hours of a business's operation, have worth. It is accepted that current hours of work have worth – workers are paid for hours of work

delivered. But future hours of work also have worth –
when you make a purchase using a credit card, you are
paying with future hours of work, which can also be
described as future earnings. You can buy, sell, and trade
future earnings today.

Thus, we make the following definitions of worth:

*1. An individual's worth is equal to the sum of the worth of
the individual's tangible assets and the worth of the
individual's future earnings.*

*2. A business's worth is equal to the sum of the worth of its
tangible assets and the worth of its future earnings.*

We expand on businesses in a later section; for this section
we concentrate on individuals.

Applying the first definition, a college graduate, with no
tangible assets, is worth what her anticipated future income
stream is worth today. The worth of a future income
stream can be said to be the amount of money in the bank
that would generate the same stream of income. If the
college graduate expects to make $25,000 a year for the
rest of her life, her current worth is the amount of money
that can generate $25,000 a year, or around $250,000,
assuming money can earn 10% interest.

A retired person, with $250,000 in the bank and no
anticipated future income, is thus also worth $250,000.

Good news. By adopting this philosophy, the college
graduate, who by most common definitions has zero
monetary worth, suddenly has $250,000 of monetary worth.

Bad news. This worth takes into account all the graduate's future earnings, so it somehow applies a figure of worth to the rest of her life. If nothing else changes, the graduate would go through life always worth about $250,000, slowly consuming some earnings and converting other earnings into tangible assets. If the graduate borrowed heavily and spent all that worth in one year, she would have no money left for the rest of her life.

More good news. Though this definition of worth covers a whole lifetime, *this worth can be changed.* Anything that alters the worth of the college graduate's future earnings or tangible assets (up or down) will alter her current worth.

Increasing the worth of future earnings

What happens if the college graduate goes to graduate school? Let's say graduate school costs $50,000, and increases her anticipated future income to $50,000 per year. She is now worth $500,000. She has gained $250,000 of worth for the price of $50,000, a net gain of $200,000.

Can this increase in worth be spent? Yes. When she commits to going to graduate school, the student can take out a school loan, and spend some of this new future worth to attend graduate school.

From where does this increase in worth come? With a little reflection, the gain in worth comes from an increase in the *value of the graduate's time.*

A scientist is taught that physical things obey a "law of conservation" – matter cannot be created or destroyed, only altered. New matter must come from some transformation of old matter, with no loss.

However, the *value* of the graduate's time is not a physical thing; it is a "market" thing. It has no mass or momentum. It does not obey physical laws. It obeys "market" laws. And it is not against market laws for value to change.

Although we present no proof, we assert that an increase in the value of a person's time (and in their worth) does not subtract from someone else's worth. The worth is *created*. It is not transferred.

In summary:

3. An individual's worth can be increased by increasing the value of the individual's time, thus increasing the worth of future earnings. This increase in worth does not subtract from someone else's worth. It is created.

How can the value of an individual's time be increased?

Three ways of increasing the value of an individual's time (in other words, an individual's productivity) come to mind.

A) An individual can acquire a better tool, which makes him more productive. (A carpenter who discards a hand saw and buys a power saw increases the value of his future earnings).

B) An individual can adopt a better process, or learn something new, which makes him more productive. (A plumber who discovers that cutting pipe on site will save him 10% of his time increases the value of his future earnings).

C) An individual can team up with other individuals, making all the individuals more productive. (A person good at hunting and a person good at gathering vegetables will be more productive working together than working separately).

Three ways of gaining productivity from teams come to mind.

a) If two (or more) individuals have mismatched skills, they can specialize. A good hunter can hunt all day and a good vegetable gatherer can gather all day.

b) Two (or more) individuals can gain from economies of scale. Even if their skills are the same, one person can shop for two people, and one person can cook for two people, and each will gain productivity.

c) Two (or more) individuals can gain from reinforcement. Because humans are social, working side by side often makes people more productive.

Summarizing:

4. The value of an individual's time, and therefore the individual's worth, can be increased by the individual
>   *joining a team with mismatched skills,*
>   *joining a team with economies of scale,*
>   *joining a team with reinforcement,*
>   *acquiring better tools, or*
>   *acquiring better knowledge and processes.*

Who gets to keep the extra worth?

When one person increases her worth by buying a tool or going to school, she gets to keep all of the gain. When a group of people increase their worth by forming a team, who gets to keep the gain?

We struggled with this question, and did not discover an answer until reading a New York Times article about William Vickrey, the late Nobel laureate economist from Columbia. The article talked about Vickrey's theories of efficient auctions, where the winner of a closed-bid auction should pay what the second highest bidder bids.

The answer to who gets to keep the extra worth generated by a team is fascinating:

5. The owner or organizer of a team gets to keep all the leftover team worth, after paying other team members for being on the team. Theoretically, in a sellers market, the owner must pay each team member $1 more than the second richest rival team can afford to pay. In a buyers market, the owner can hire each team member for $1 less than the second cheapest rival team member can afford to participate for.

Several examples are in order.

A doctor earns $50 per hour. A housecleaner has expenses of $5 per hour. The doctor hires the housecleaner for one hour per week, at $10 per hour, making a temporary team of two. Assuming the doctor gets to work one more hour, $45 of worth is being created each week by the team. The doctor is keeping $40 of the extra worth; the housecleaner $5.

There are three doctors, earning respectively $80, $60, and $50 per hour. There is only one housecleaner available for one hour, with expenses of $5 per hour. The $80 doctor will hire the housecleaner for $60, and the other doctors will do their own housecleaning. $75 of worth is being created, the doctor is keeping $20, and the housecleaner is keeping $55.

There is one doctor, earning $50 per hour. There are three housecleaners, with expenses respectively of $9, $7, and $5 per hour. The doctor will hire the $5 housecleaner for $7 per hour. $45 of worth is being created, the doctor is keeping $43, and the housecleaner is keeping $2.

An owner-manager forms a business by hiring five other workers. The business makes a profit of $200 per hour, after non-labor expenses. Because of market forces, the owner-manager must pay the workers $30, $30, $20, $10, and $10 per hour. The owner-manager gets to keep the remaining $100 per hour.

A non-working owner forms a similar business by hiring a manager and five workers. The business also makes a profit of $200 per hour, after non-labor expenses. Because of market forces, the owner must pay the manager $70 per hour, and must pay the workers the same $30, $30, $20, $10, and $10 per hour. The owner gets to keep the remaining $30 per hour.

It is interesting to note that an efficient business can afford to pay an employee more than a less-efficient business can. This is because:

6. The same employee generates more worth for an efficient business than for a less-efficient business.

Increasing the worth of tangible assets

Since the worth of an individual is equal to the sum of the worth of tangible assets and the worth of future earnings, an individual's worth can also be increased by increasing the worth of his tangible assets. This can be done by exchanging some of his assets for other assets that are worth more.

By exchanging assets we mean buying and selling, or trading. In voluntary trades (as opposed to some form of theft), both sides gain worth, else the trade would not take place.

How do both sides gain?

Assume there are two parties in a trade. Again using the argument that value does not obey the laws of physics, an item can be worth a different amount to each of the two parties. By moving from one party to another, the value of an item increases; therefore worth is created. Both sides share this worth.

One example of trade is barter. A hunter gives a farmer a rabbit in return for a basket of turnips. To the hunter, the rabbit is worth one hour of time; the basket of turnips two hours of time. To the farmer, the basket of turnips is worth one hour of time; the rabbit two hours of time. The trade creates one hunter-hour plus one farmer-hour of worth, with each party sharing part of the created worth.

Money is somehow a neutral facilitator of bartering that allows one half of a barter to take place independently of the other half. Using the concept of money, the example can be restated as a sale. A hunter has a rabbit that is worth $10 to him and worth $20 to a farmer. The hunter sells the rabbit to the farmer for $15. Both the hunter and the farmer gain $5 of worth.

How is the gain divided?

Market forces determine how a gain in worth from trade is divided. Market forces can best be illustrated by further examples.

There are three hunters, each with a similar rabbit, and one farmer, who wants a rabbit. To the farmer, a rabbit is worth $20. To the hunters, their rabbits are worth $10, $12, and $15 respectively. The farmer buys a rabbit from the first hunter for $12. $10 of worth is created; the hunter gets $2 of the gain, and the farmer gets $8 of the gain.

There is one hunter with a rabbit worth $10 to him. There are three farmers, each of whom wants the rabbit. The rabbit is worth $15, $18, and $20 respectively to the farmers. The hunter sells the third farmer the rabbit for $18. $10 of worth is created; the hunter gets $8 of the gain, the farmer gets $2 of the gain.

Summarizing:

7. Both parties gain worth in a voluntary sale or trade, because items change value when they change ownership. The distribution of the gain in worth is determined by market forces.

What assets have value?

Assets that meet needs have value (food, shelter, clothing). Assets that are tools that increase the value of an individual's time, or save an individual time, have value (powered lawn mowers, cars, college educations). Belonging to teams has an important effect on the value of an individual's time, so assets that improve team cohesion have value (sporting events, club memberships, social skills).

Since owning or organizing a team has the largest effect on the value of an individual's time, assets that facilitate leadership have great value. Management training comes to mind; however, the assets that have the largest affect on an individual's leadership position are *status symbols*.

People, among their many instincts, have both the instinct to lead teams, and the instinct to follow team leaders. Both these instincts somehow recognize status symbols. The earliest descriptions of tribal leaders note the trinkets and doodads the leaders possessed. Today, the better-dressed person, or the person with the nicer car, gets more respect.

What makes a status symbol

Rarity. No matter how much value an item adds to a person's time, if everybody has it, it cannot denote position. The rarer an item is, the fewer people there are that can posses a copy, and the higher an individual's position must be for that individual to posses a copy. If only one purple robe exists, only the highest-ranking person will have one. The robe will then identify that person's position to the instincts of her followers.

Showing a status symbol is the slightly more civilized equivalent of flexing your muscles or baring your teeth, to demonstrate economic power.

To summarize:

8. Assets that provide for needs, multiply the worth of time, or denote leadership position have worth, in roughly that order. Assets have different worth for different people.

Businesses

We restate our previous definition: a business's worth is equal to the sum of the worth of its tangible assets and the worth of its future earnings.

Stock

Since a share of stock represents a fraction of the ownership of a business, the same assertion holds for a single share of stock: the worth of a share of stock is equal to the sum of the worth of the assets per share, and the worth of future earnings per share. A business with $10 worth of assets per share, which earns an unchanging $2 per year per share, is worth ($10 + $20) per share, or $30 per share (assuming $2 per year is worth $20, which is the amount of money in the bank at 10% interest needed to generate the $2 per year).

Growing and shrinking

A business with no assets that earns $2 per year per share, and whose earnings increase at a constant 5% per year, is theoretically worth the amount of money in a bank that can generate the same growing income stream, or $40 per share, assuming the money in the bank gets 10% interest.

Likewise, the same business with earnings decreasing at a constant 5% per year is worth $13.33 per share.

The same business that earns $2 per year per share, and whose earnings increase at a constant 15% per year, is theoretically worth an infinite amount, because no amount of money in the bank at 10% interest can generate a yearly stream of earnings that grows this fast.

There are practical limits on size and lifespan, however – a business that grows too large becomes inefficient and a business that exists too long becomes sclerotic.

Growth is important

Company assets	Earnings per share	Growth per year	Worth per share*
$0	$2	0	$20
$0	$2	5%	$40
$0	$2	-5%	$13.33

* assumes an interest rate of 10% (for lower interest rates, growth is more important)

Worth, value, and price

Since the theoretical worth of a share of stock is unknown in real life, each owner places her own value on a share of stock.

These owner values differ, for three main reasons. First, although the law ensures all owners have access to information needed to make good estimates, this access costs time (and therefore money), and so is self-rationed by each owner. Second, even with the same access to information, experienced owners make better estimates than inexperienced owners. Third, similar owners pursuing different investment strategies will place different values on the same share of stock.

Thus, three concepts exist for each share of stock – the (unknown) theoretical worth of the share, the value each owner places on the share, and the price of the share, determined by market forces acting on the set of owner values.

To note

It is interesting to note that as bank interest rates drop to zero, using our definition of worth, all individuals and companies approach an infinite worth. At this time, we do not fully understand the implications of this observation, or what the countering forces are.

It is also interesting to note that instead of using a theoretical amount of money in the bank to assign a value to an income stream ($2 per year = $20 in the bank), we can use a theoretical amount of money invested in the stock market ($2 per year = $? in the stock market). We do not understand the implications of this, either.

Formulas used

The worth of a stream of future earnings is equal to the amount of money in a bank which, multiplied by the interest rate, will produce the earnings stream.

$$m \times i = e$$
$$m = e/i$$

where

e = yearly earnings
i = yearly interest rate
m = money in bank for yearly earnings

The worth of a *growing* stream of future earnings is equal to the sum of two amounts of money in a bank. One amount multiplied by the interest rate will produce the non-growing earnings stream. The other amount multiplied by the interest rate will increase both amounts of money in the bank by the growth rate.

$$m_e \times i = e$$
$$m_e = e/i$$

$$m_g \times i = (m_e + m_g) \times g$$
$$(m_g \times i) - (m_g \times g) = m_e \times g$$
$$m_g \times (i - g) = m_e \times g$$
$$m_g = m_e \times g/(i - g)$$

$$m = m_e + m_g$$
$$m = m_e + (m_e \times g/(i - g))$$
$$m = m_e \times (1 + g/(i - g))$$
$$m = e/i \times (1 + g/(i - g))$$

where

e = yearly earnings
g = growth rate of yearly earnings (where $g < i$)
i = yearly interest rate
m_e = money in bank for non-growing yearly earnings
m_g = money in bank for growth of money in bank
m = total money in bank for growing yearly earnings

Starting and growing a business

One way to start a business is as follows. A single organizer, or group of organizers, forms a team. This team has worth – the worth of its future earnings. The organizers sell some of this worth in the form of stock. The organizers use the proceeds of the sale to operate the business until the business earns enough to cover day-to-day operations.

In another case, a business decides to grow. The planned growth adds worth to the business. The business sells some of this worth in the form of bonds or new stock, and funds the planned growth with the proceeds.

Owners benefit most

Because the owner or organizer of a team gets to keep excess team worth, and because it usually (though not always) takes money to form a new business team, the already rich are usually the ones who end up owning, and therefore benefiting the most, from new businesses. Thus, as the cliché states, the rich get richer.

Actually, since for one person to acquire more worth (without using force), everybody he deals with must also gain worth, a more accurate cliché would be:

The rich get richer faster.

Inheritance taxes

Most countries impose high inheritance taxes. Like a firebreak, inheritance taxes diminish the rich-get-richer-faster spiral as it tries to move from generation to generation.

Positive and negative competition

The drive to become rich seems to be fueled by the instincts to beat competitors and to lead teams. These instincts are strong, and manifest themselves in two forms: moving ahead faster than competitors (positive competition), or holding competitors back (negative competition).

Since creating worth is not a zero-sum game, these two manifestations do not produce the same result. If an individual or business, and their competitors, are creating worth as fast as they can, and one pulls ahead, this is good for the economy as a whole. Worth is being created at a maximum rate. If an individual or business is somehow preventing their competitors from creating worth as fast as they can, some potential worth is not being created. The economy grows slower than it could.

Holding others back may or may not be intentional. One example of holding others back is that if some resource useful for acquiring worth is limited, the first group to become rich can monopolize that resource. In effect, they shut the door behind themselves, intentionally or not. Up until the nineteenth century, land was often the limiting resource for creating worth, and ownership of land often divided the rich from the not rich.

Self regulation

Honest businesses want to do no harm (e.g., pollute, exploit workers, or produce dangerous products). If doing no harm adds cost, businesses self-regulate, or help the government write regulations, to prevent dishonest companies gaining an unfair cost advantage by doing harm. Self regulation is good.

Greed, profit, and shareholder value

Greedy companies chase profit and short-term shareholder value. A better goal for a company is to maximize customer happiness divided by production cost. The higher this ratio is compared to the same ratio of a company's competitors, the more profit a company will make.

10. Ironically, maximum profit comes not from maximizing profit, but from maximizing customer happiness divided by production cost (H/C).

Natural history

When our world was created, it was imbued with the principle of *the survival of the fittest*. It was also imbued with the principle of *the fitness of the whole is greater than the sum of the fitness of the parts*. Guided by these two principles, life evolved "upward" toward ever better organisms and teams. Bacteria combined into cells, cells combined into plants and animals, and animals combined into hives, schools, flocks, herds, and packs. Random mutations that led to better groups survived; those that led to worse groups disappeared.

Human history

We humans continued, and continue, upward evolution. We invented tribes and chiefs, then agriculture, villages, cities, kingdoms, and empires, then industry, nations, and presidents.

Religions that lead us closer to a balance of strength, meekness, punishment, forgiveness, thrift and charity thrive (with the societies they support). Religions that lead us toward belligerence and revenge, or toward defensive weakness and tolerance of wrong, or toward debt, wither (with the societies they support).

Legal incorporation and stock markets are inventions that greatly aided the formation of businesses – the current epitome of worth-generating teams.

Each culture's list of heroes – kings, religious figures, inventors, culture shapers, generals, and recently business tycoons – traces the path of that culture's increase in team worth.

In summary:

11. History is the story of the evolution of increasingly synergistic organisms and teams, due to the interworking principles of "the survival of the fittest" and "the fitness of the whole is greater than the sum of the fitness of the parts".

Reverse teams

Democratic cities, states, and nations (and clubs and cooperatives, too) are teams of a special sort. They are *reverse teams*. A business pays team members for providing services to the business. In a reverse team such as a nation, however, team members pay the team for providing services to the team members.

Reverse teams create worth, or they wouldn't exist. They create worth directly and indirectly.

Directly, reverse teams use economy of scale to provide services to team members at a cost less than the cost team members would pay separately for the services. For example, all the citizens in a town pool tax money and buy new roads for $1 million. If the total price would have been $1.5 million if each citizen built their own section of road, $500,000 of worth is created by the town. Cooperatives also work on this principle.

Indirectly, reverse teams provide a framework within which businesses and individuals can operate more efficiently, therefore generating more worth for themselves. Inter-business teams, and even businesses themselves, must operate within some framework of laws and processes. Cities, states, and nations provide such frameworks. A portion of the worth created within the frameworks is taxed to operate the government; the rest is kept by the companies. Again, all parties gain.

In summary:

12. Reverse teams, such as cooperatives and democratic countries, create worth directly through economies of scale, and indirectly by providing a framework in which other teams can create worth. They are financed by a tax on a portion of the created worth.

Trade deficit

Running a trade deficit is not bad in itself. Both countries gain worth in every non-forced trade. It is what a country does with the created worth that determines winners and losers.

13. A trade deficit is not bad in itself. All countries gain worth from trading. The country that best reinvests its trade gains in new worth-generating capital is the country that wins, regardless of the direction of money flow.

Evolving economic ideas

Adam Smith (1723-1790)
The Wealth of Nations, Book I

Chapter I
The greatest improvement in the productive powers of labour ... seem to have been the effects of the division of labour.

Chapter II
It is not from the benevolence of the butcher, the brewer, or the baker, that we expect our dinner, but from their regard to their own interest.

Adam Smith published 'The Wealth of Nations' in 1776, the same year the American Declaration of Independence was signed.

David Ricardo (1772-1823)
Principles of Political Economy and Taxation

Chapter VII
Though she [Portugal] could make the cloth with the labour of 90 men, she would import it from a country [England] where it required the labour of 100 men to produce it, because it would be advantageous to her rather to employ her capital in the production of wine, for which she would obtain more cloth from England, than she could produce by diverting a portion of her capital from the cultivation of vines to the manufacture of cloth.

Ricardo's (often misinterpreted) law of comparative advantage says a country benefits most from specializing in what it does best relative to itself, not in what it does best relative to the countries it trades with.

Karl Marx (1818-1883)
Value, Price, And Profit: An Introduction to the Theory of Capitalism

Chapter VI. Value and Labor
Yet, *its [a commodity's] value remaining always the same*, … it must be something distinct from, and independent of, these *different rates of exchange* with different articles.

If we consider *commodities as values*, we consider them exclusively under the single aspect of *realized, fixed*, or, if you like, *crystallized social labor*. … But how does one measure *quantities of labor*? By the *time the labor lasts*, in measuring the labor by the hour, the day, etc.

Chapter X. Profit is made by Selling a Commodity at its Value
The value of a commodity is determined by the *total quantity of labor* contained in it. … Part of the labor contained in the commodity is *paid* labor; part is *unpaid* labor. By selling, therefore, the commodity *at its value*, that is, as the crystallization of the *total quantity of labor* bestowed upon it, the capitalist must necessarily sell it at a profit. He sells not only what has cost him an equivalent, but he sells also what has cost him nothing, although it has cost his workman labor. … I repeat, therefore, that normal and average profits are made by selling commodities not *above*, but *at their real values*.

Chapter XIV. The Struggle between Capital and Labor and its Results
Trades Unions work well as centers of resistance against the encroachments of capital. They fail partially from an

injudicious use of their power. They fail generally from limiting themselves to a guerrilla war against the effects of the existing system, instead of simultaneously trying to change it, instead of using their organized forces as a lever for the final emancipation of the working class, that is to say, the ultimate abolition of the wage system.

Karl Marx believed a commodity's value derives from man-hours. We agree. However, we assert that Karl Marx's belief that each commodity and man-hour has a single value (instead of changing its value with a change of ownership) led him to the misguided conclusion that profit derives only from the difference between a worker's output and his wages. This conclusion, in turn, led to a further miscalculation of the benefit of the emancipation of workers.

William Vickrey (1914-1996)

Vickrey showed that Dutch descending-price open-bid auctions, and sealed-bid auctions in which the winner pays the price that was bid, are equivalent. He also showed that English ascending-price open-bid auctions, and sealed-bid auctions in which the winner pays the second-highest price that was bid (called Vickrey auctions), are equivalent.

Though auctions are not the topic of this book, Vickrey's ideas are enlightening. The idea that the person who places the highest value on an item need pay only one dollar more than the amount the person who places the second-highest value on the item is willing to pay is an important part of understanding the creation of worth.

John Nash (1928-2015)

John Nash shared the 1994 Nobel Prize in Economic Sciences for his "pioneering analysis of equilibria in the theory of non-cooperative games".

We interpret Nash's work as showing that the benefits to society of Adam Smith's "invisible hand" of self-interest can become stuck at local maximi, and that cooperation is needed to move beyond these so-called Nash equilibria.

Thus, for society to benefit most, competition and cooperation must co-exist. For example, modern economic competition is bounded by rules we all agree on. No violence, no stealing, no cheating, no lying. If enough of us start breaking these rules, all of us must adversely adjust our behavior out of self-interest, collectively sinking to a lower Nash equilibrium, to the detriment of society.

Chapter III

Five Principles of God

A Religious Essay

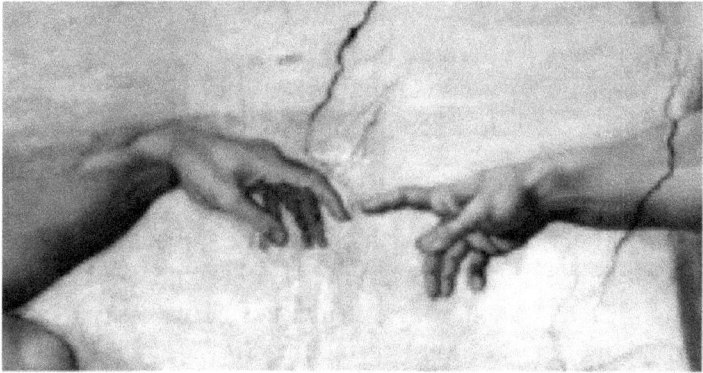

(detail of) The Creation of Adam (1512, fresco)
Michelangelo di Lodovico Buonarroti Simonl
(1475-1564) Italian painter, sculptor, architect.

Religion is personal

Critically accepting ideas and critically rejecting ideas are both powerful learning techniques. The personal religious opinions in this chapter will not be widely accepted. Hopefully they will be thought provoking.

Troika

As science and philosophy progress, so, too, does religion, as we steadily learn more about God. In the long run science, philosophy, and religion advance together to pull our species forward like three horses of a Russian sleigh.

In the beginning

When God created the Earth about four and a half billion years ago, He imbued it with physical laws, economic principles, and evolutionary principles. This essay focuses on two of God's economic principles (*invisible hand* and *Nash agreement*) and three of God's evolutionary principles (*survival of the fittest*, *team fitness*, and *team niceness*).

Three principles apply to all life

In his book "The Wealth of Nations", Adam Smith describes an economic principle that he calls the *invisible hand*. When individuals work for their own selfish gain, the community benefits.

In his book "Origin of Species", Charles Darwin describes a principle of evolution nowadays called *survival of the fittest*. Fitter individuals survive more often and produce more offspring; less fit individuals survive less often and produce fewer offspring.

The economics chapter of this book describes a second principle of evolution – that the fitness of the whole is greater than the sum of the fitness of the parts (which we here call *team fitness*). Individuals that are team members are more fit than individuals that are not team members.

These three principles, working together, drive all life to evolve into ever more complex teams. When God created the first self-replicating RNA between three and a half and four billion years ago (some scientists posit He used volcano-heated pools of organic chemicals, others that He used chemical reactions in clay crystals), these three principles took over and drove RNA to evolve into bacteria with DNA, bacteria into cells, cells into plants and animals, and animals into hives, schools, flocks, herds, and packs.

Two principles apply to intelligent life

Our pre-human ancestors evolved hands and three-dimensional visualization swinging through trees. They walked onto the African Savanna on two legs, where they evolved the use of tools with their free hands. To better coordinate teams of tool users, our ancestors evolved speech.

We assume (without evidence) that speech, tool-based team hunting, and tool-based team warfare evolved in lockstep, progress in one driving progress in the others.

Regardless, with the evolution of speech came the ability to make verbal agreements. And just as importantly, came the ability to break verbal agreements. We define intelligence in a species as the ability to make, keep, and break verbal agreements.

We choose this odd definition of intelligence because when a species evolves the ability to make, keep, and break verbal agreements, two more of God's principles kick in – *Nash agreement* and *team niceness*.

Metaphorically, this point in our history is represented (in Western culture) by Pandora's box opening, by the fall from Heaven of the archangel Satan, and by Eve taking a bite from the apple of knowledge.

This is because these two principles, unlike the first three, do not automatically pull evolution in the direction of better teams. Rather, they produce a tension between team progress and team regression – more specifically between good and evil.

Nash agreement

John Nash was a mathematician who was depicted in the movie "A Beautiful Mind". He won a Nobel prize in economics for describing a theory we simplistically call *Nash agreement*, and simplistically interpret as follows. Nash claimed that the maximum benefit for a community does not come from selfish behavior (Adam Smith's *invisible hand*) alone. Maximum benefit comes from a combination of competition and agreement. In other words, from bounded competition.

A community that competes, but agrees not to kill, lie, cheat, or steal will benefit more than a community that allows law-of-the-jungle competition, and will benefit more than a community that stifles competition.

For example, the ten commandments are a *Nash agreement*.

Team niceness

If two teams of the same size and ability compete, the meaner team wins. Of two teams, the nicer (meeker) team retains more members and is therefore larger.

Biological tension

Once a species can make, keep, and break verbal agreements, tension in biological evolution exists at the individual level and the team level.

At the individual level, if everyone honors a *Nash agreement*, everyone benefits. If everyone breaks a *Nash agreement*, everyone suffers. If everybody except one person honors a *Nash agreement*, everyone benefits, but the cheater benefits most. Keeping agreements conveys evolutionary fitness, and breaking agreements conveys evolutionary fitness.

At the team level, a small team is tempted to be mean to win; a large team is compelled to be nice to keep itself together. Mean conveys evolutionary fitness, and nice conveys evolutionary fitness.

Biological handoff

If we evolved a genetic compulsion to be nice, the first person with a mutation in the niceness gene would end up ruling the world and having many children. If we evolved a genetic compulsion to be mean, the first team with a mutation in the meanness gene would become large enough to rule the world and have many children.

If niceness and meanness were left to the rational part of our brains, we would be superficially nice, but would stab each other in the back for a nickel's gain.

How did biology handle this good vs. evil impasse? The answer is fascinating.

To break this impasse, biology evolved the conscience – a part of the brain controlled neither by genetic urges, nor by rational decisions. Instead, this part of the brain acts as a sort of moral inertia, and is influenced by parents, priests, and peers. Sigmund Freud called this part of the brain the super-ego.

We call what goes into the conscience religion. Religion evolves. Thus, because it valued the benefits of large teams, but could not break the impasse of good and evil through genetic control, biology passed the evolutionary baton to religion:

In species that can speak, biology passes the job of mediating good and evil to religious evolution.

Religion brings us closer to God

Religion, improving through millennia of trial and error, brings us gradually closer to understanding God and God's Word. God tells us to damp some biological urges and amplify others. He conveys non-intuitive rules and practices for getting along peacefully and productively with others. His love and guidance allow us, despite being a product of His evolutionary principles, to live bountifully in nations of millions.

Do we have a choice what goes into our consciences?

Yes and no. Yes in the sense that we as a society can put anything we want into the consciences of our children. But God made this competitive world in such a way that if our society does not choose to put a good understanding of Him into the consciences of our children, then we will be conquered or bought by a society that puts a better understanding of God into the consciences of its children.

In other words:

Societies with the better understanding of God win.

In the past, when land was important, societies with the better understanding of God won militarily. Today, since land is no longer the primary source of income, societies with the better understanding of God win financially.

God and science

To build bridges, spaceships, and computer chips, and to predict weather and planetary motion, scientists continually improve their understanding of the physical laws of God.

To build politically and financially healthy, militarily strong, and law-abiding societies, parents, politicians, and priests continually improve their understanding of the God that goes into the consciences of our children.

Our consciences are quirky. As we humans struggle to advance through the religious stages of nature worship, multiple gods, a single wrathful God, wise sages, and a single stern, loving and forgiving God, we wrap our hard-won understanding of God in religious ritual and history, to better fit the way our consciences function.

Unfortunately, some ritual and history that helped our consciences in the past does not help in the present, because it conflicts with scientific understanding.

We need both God and science for society to work. If we throw either away, a society that better integrates God and science will conquer or buy our society. That is how God made biologic and religious evolution work.

Consequently, as we advance religiously, and disentangle ourselves from ritual and history that has outlived its usefulness, we must be careful not to throw the Baby out with the bath water – we must keep and build on our understanding of the stern, loving, and forgiving God that keeps our society healthy, unconquered, and unbought.

Can religion be used to manipulate a population?

Yes. A society, like an individual, has choice. It can choose a religion that manipulates its own citizens. But the true God empowers. So a society that chooses self-manipulation will be conquered or bought by a society that chooses to move closer to God, and practice a religion that empowers its citizens.

Can religion be used to conquer others?

Yes. A Society can choose a religion that conquers other societies. But the true God defends and enriches. So a society that chooses to conquer will eventually be defeated by societies that choose to move closer to God, and practice religions that encourage defensive alliances and wealth creation.

However, a society with no religion will lose to a society with a conquering religion.

Being in debt is a sin

We have learned through trial and error that when God talks about usury, He does not mean all loans are bad, and He does not mean all loans are good. Being in debt, *other than for low-risk capital improvement at a fair interest rate*, is a sin. Lending money to someone, *other than for low-risk capital improvement at a fair interest rate*, is a sin.

God will forgive this sin if you have a change of heart, and start working your way out of debt. He is understanding of special circumstances. But if you are unrepentant, and die in debt, or having voted to put your organization in debt, there is a good chance you will end up in Hell.

Chasing profit is a sin

Making a profit is not a sin. Accumulating profit, and becoming wealthy, even very wealthy, is not a sin. But explicitly *chasing* profit (or shareholder value, for a company) *is* a sin. This is called greed. There is a subtle distinction between wealth and greed, and it has to do with how decisions are made.

God made this competitive world in such a way that helping others creates worth. If a company sets a goal of maximizing helping others in some manner, then decisions guided by this goal will lead to helping others, and the company will maximize the amount of money it earns over the long term. This is good.

Paradoxically, if a company sets a goal of maximizing the amount of money it earns, then decisions guided by this goal will often maximize short term profit, at the expense of the company's long term ability to help others, and the company will slowly spiral downward, earning less and less money over the long term. This is not good.

The Devil made me solve it

On the path to God, engineering problems are to be solved and social issues are to be navigated. If the Devil cannot convert you to evil, he may tempt you down the wayward path of trying to solve a social issue, instead of trying to navigate it.

Depth in philosophy

A little philosophy inclineth man's mind to atheism, but depth in philosophy bringeth men's minds about to religion. *Francis Bacon (1561-1626), English renaissance author, statesman, philosopher.*

Chapter IV

Hectosophy

A New Writing Form

The Alchymist, in Search of the Philosopher's Stone
(1771, oil on canvas)
Joseph Wright of Derby (1734-1797) English painter.

The story of accumulism

The preceding three chapters present ideas evolved *using* the philosophy of accumulism.

This and the remaining chapters of this book present the story of the *development* of accumulism.

An honest but impossible goal

In 1995, as stated in the introduction, I set a goal of speeding up software development by a factor of ten. I was curious about what would happen if I made an honest effort to solve an impossible problem.

I concluded most decisions made by software developers are based on experience, and cannot be proven correct by formal analysis.

Not knowing how else to improve an experienced-based endeavor, I started collecting software development ideas in a journal. This helped, and I became interested in "collecting ideas" as a way to learn.

The inventor's paradox

In his book "How to Solve It", Hungarian Mathematician George Pólya (1887-1985) lists many ways to solve problems.

For some problems, he says, it is paradoxically easier to first solve a more general problem and then use the general solution to solve the original problem, than it is to solve the original problem directly. He calls this the inventor's paradox.

For example, before solving the problem 193 + 325, it might be easier to first solve the general problem of how to add any two integers together, and then use that knowledge to solve the original problem.

For me, speeding up software development was an inventor's paradox. I discovered I made the fastest progress if I spent most of my time working on a more general problem.

Thus I gradually switched from pursuing one goal to pursuing two goals:

(The general problem) Figure out how best to collect ideas in a journal to improve an experienced-based endeavor.

(The specific problem) Speed up software development by a factor of ten.

Patterns

In 1996 I stumbled on the pattern writing form.

American architect and author Christopher Alexander (1936-) introduced this writing form in his book "A Pattern Language", in 1977, as a way to record and communicate good architecture practices.

Alexander defines a pattern as a written description a few pages long that has a specific form, including a unique title. The pattern outlines a problem that involves a set of opposing forces, and suggests a good solution. Alexander defines a pattern language as a collection of patterns.

As Alexander uses it, the term "pattern" refers to both a writing form and the content of the form, as do the terms essay, short story, novel, dissertation, and scientific-journal article.

Starting in the early 1990s, American software developer and inventor Ward Cunningham (1949-), American software developer and author Kent Beck (1961-), and others started using the pattern writing form to record and communicate good software practices.

Example

The following simple example pattern was copied from *http://en.wikipedia.org/wiki/Pattern_language (02/27/2014).*

Name: **ChocolateChipRatio**
Context: You are baking chocolate chip cookies in small batches for family and friends
Consider these patterns first: SugarRatio, FlourRatio, EggRatio
Problem: Determine the optimum ratio of chocolate chips to cookie dough
Solution: Observe that most people consider chocolate to be the best part of the chocolate chip cookie. Also observe that too much chocolate may prevent the cookie from holding together, decreasing its appeal. Since you are cooking in small batches, cost is not a consideration. Therefore, use the maximum amount of chocolate chips that results in a really sturdy cookie.
Consider next: NutRatio or CookingTime or FreezingMethod

To Capture Knowledge

British software developer and author Martin Fowler (1963-), on his website *http://www.martinfowler.com/articles/writingPatterns.html (02/27/2014)* states:

A common complaint about patterns books is that they have nothing new to tell experienced developers. Not just is this true, but it's the whole point of patterns. Patterns are there to capture knowledge from the field, not to present original ideas.

Named paragraphs

I found the pattern writing form useful. But I wanted a writing form that helped systematically improve ideas. I borrowed the concept of naming my ideas, and continued to experiment.

Instead of collecting ideas in my journal, I now collected named paragraphs in my journal.

Finite collections of named paragraphs

In 1999 I discovered that it helped to occasionally summarize the ideas in my journal into a set of one hundred named paragraphs, or a set of ten named paragraphs.

This was an important discovery – the difference between how to choose patterns for a pattern language, and how to choose good personal ideas.

Patterns are chosen because several people use the pattern. If several people use it, it must have merit.

However, it is hard to judge the merit of a personal subjective idea. Instead,

Personal ideas are best judged relative to each other.

I found I could force the judgment of personal ideas relative to each other if I occasionally reduced the size of my collection of named paragraphs to a fixed number, using the same number every time. This created a "survival of the fittest" mechanism for my ideas.

With a target size of one hundred, for example, each reduction would keep the top one hundred named paragraphs. The collection would gradually improve in quality, not quantity.

The numbers one hundred, and ten, are not magic numbers. The concept of occasional reduction will work with any fixed size. I considered sizes of seven, one dozen, twenty, and sixty – all common collection sizes in our culture – before I settled on a size of one hundred for big collections, and ten for small collections.

The sizes of five, and twenty, also seem to help me occasionally.

Decasophies and Hectosophies

For convenience, the following words are defined:

decasophy (de kas' ə fee)
noun: A collection of ten subjective ideas, observations, practices, rules, or techniques.
From the Greek "deca" meaning ten, and "sophy" meaning knowledge or wisdom.

hectosophy (hek tos' ə fee)
noun: A collection of one hundred subjective ideas, observations, practices, rules, or techniques. Sometimes composed of ten decasophies.
From the Greek "hecto" meaning one hundred, and "sophy" meaning knowledge or wisdom.

Single author

When reducing the size of a collection of subjective ideas, personal judgment is used to decide which ideas to keep, and which to discard. Therefore a hectosophy, or

decasophy, has only one author – the person who choses
the ideas.

1999 hectosophy-based learning approach
When I started using hectosophies, I followed this learning
approach.

1. *Set an ambitious, motivating goal.*
2. *Try many things and record what worked.*
3. *Occasionally summarize what worked into a
   hectosophy or decasophy.*

Everything looks like a nail
If you have a hammer, everything looks like a nail.

Between 1999 and 2009, I used hectosophies and
decasophies to record and summarize software
development ideas, learning ideas, economic ideas, and
religious ideas. I found my personal understanding
improved in each of these fields.

In other words, hectosophy-based learning helped me
increase subjective understanding.

During this decade I also recorded and summarized
efficiency and people skill ideas. However, I did not
improve in these fields. In fact, I made negative progress.
My 1999 hectosophy-based learning approach hurt my self-
improvement.

Chapter V

Preserving Free Will

Using Hectosophies for Self-Improvement

Erasmus of Rotterdam (1523, oil and tempera on wood)
Hans Holbein the Younger *(c. 1497-1543), German artist and printmaker.*

Perplexed labyrinth

Among the many difficulties in Holy Scripture – and there are many of them – none presents a more perplexed labyrinth than the problem of the freedom of the will.
Desiderius Erasmus Roterodamus *(1466-1536), Dutch humanist, priest, and theologian.*

My struggle, 2009 to 2016

As mentioned in the previous chapter, between 1999 and 2009 I succeeded when I used my hectosophy-based learning approach to improve subjective understanding, and I failed soundly when I attempted to use it for self-improvement.

I became intrigued and stubborn. Why did hectosophies help some learning and hinder other learning? I wanted to see if I could make hectosophies a safe tool for all subjective learning.

Do each iteration differently

In 2009, I had my first useful insight. I realized that settling on one way to do a repeating task eliminated trial and error. Eliminating trial and error slowed learning.

So for repeating tasks I wanted to improve, I resolved to

Do each iteration of a repeating task differently for the rest of my life.

I didn't start brushing my teeth differently each day, but I did start varying my personal daily routine, my work routine, and my participation in regular meetings I attended.

Small goals

I experimented with setting many small goals for self-improvement, instead of setting one large goal, as I did for improving understanding. This helped (although I later abandoned goals in favor of adjustment).

I switched from *improving people skills*, in general, to improving individual skills such as doing my job better, and getting along with family better.

Say <> do

Say what you will do, and then do what you said you would do. One of my small goals became getting better at saying only what I knew I could accomplish, and then accomplishing what I said I would accomplish.

I started using this technique for my varying daily routine. Each day I would say what I was going to do, and try to do it.

Two types of learning

I gradually stopped striving for one learning approach that worked for all subjective learning and improvement, and started looking for two approaches – one that worked for improving subjective understanding, and another that worked for self-improvement.

Past tense sentences

I started recording what worked using past tense sentences, instead of imperative sentences. I found that imperative sentences often became burdensome rules that that were hard to follow.

I recorded, for example, "Getting up at six o'clock in the morning helped" instead of "Get up at six o'clock in the morning".

Choices on paper

To improve making choices, I began to make subjective choices explicitly on paper, by writing down the options, the pros and cons of each option, and my choice.

"Do I stay up late to finish this paper? If I do, I will be tired. If I do not, I will have to skip exercise class tomorrow morning to finish the paper. I choose to finish the paper tonight."

Be blocked

I found that when I had a psychological block, ironically a good approach for getting over the block was to not fight it. If I continued to learn while not directly trying to reduce the block, the block often melted on its own.

For example, for a while I accepted the fact that I had a hard time getting started in the morning. Eventually I stopped having this problem.

Letting things go their own way

True mastery can be gained
By letting things go their own way.
It can't be gained by interfering.
Be content with what you have;
Rejoice in the way things are.
When you realize there is nothing lacking,
The whole world belongs to you.
*Laozi, also spelled **Lao Tzu** (circa 6th century BC), legendary Chinese sage and author of the Tao Te Ching. Translated by **Stephen Mitchell** (1943-), American translator.*

Improvement tax

While doing each task, spend a small percentage of time making long-term improvements. Tasks you spend more time on will get more improvement; tasks you spend less time on will get less improvement.

When I realized my email inbox was too full, for three months, each time I read emails, I spent one minute cleaning my inbox.

Worst first

Make the most-needed improvement first. Except if you are blocked. In that case, be blocked.

When I cleaned my room, I cleaned the messiest part first.

Count your blessings

Counting your blessings is a type of review that helps you emotionally feel what is working.

Be average on teams

I found this provocative wording helped me personally remember that the power of a team derives primarily from how smoothly it operates, and secondarily from the technical correctness of its process.

Trying to improve a team often disrupts the smoothness of the team. It is usually best if team members do their own jobs well, and try not to make waves.

Inherent words-on-paper tensions

Each of the above adjustments helped make hectosophy-based learning somewhat more useful for self-improvement, but I continued to struggle. I eventually concluded that all learning approaches, which involve *words on paper* and *people's behavior*, have a built-in tension that is very difficult to resolve.

Dogma vs. free will

The more useful words on paper are, the greater the danger they will become dogma, and interfere with future decision making.

When dealing with nature, it is okay to have one best way of doing things. When dealing with people, it is not okay.

In the sport of rock-climbing, it is okay to gradually settle on one best route up the face of a cliff – the cliff does not care, and does not change. In the sport of American football, it is not okay to gradually settle on one best play.

People do not respond the same way, each time, to the same situation – you need free will to deal with people. Likewise, your subconscious does not respond the same way, each time, to your conscious mind – you need free will to deal with yourself, too.

Understanding the difficulty

I began to understand why I was having trouble applying hectosophy-based learning to self-improvement. The difficulty was not with hectosophies per se, but rather with the paradox inherent in using words on paper to help self-improvement.

A words-on-paper learning paradox

I distilled my new understanding into the following learning paradox.

*To use words on paper for self-improvement, you must **fully** follow the words you write on paper, and you must **not** follow the words you write on paper.*

2015 hectosophy-based learning approach

By early 2015, I had changed my learning approach to the following:

1. *List ten self-improvement goals.*
2. *Make choices on paper.*
3. *Each day, state the process you will follow.*
4. *Follow it.*
5. *Record what worked.*
6. *Occasionally summarize what worked into a hectosophy or decasophy.*

I included the techniques of setting ten self-improvement goals, and of making choices on paper, to encourage free will.

I now fully followed what I wrote on paper for each day's process (which was only what I thought I could achieve), but I did not follow what I accumulated in my hectosophy.

Chapter VI

Decisions

Permanent and Ephemeral

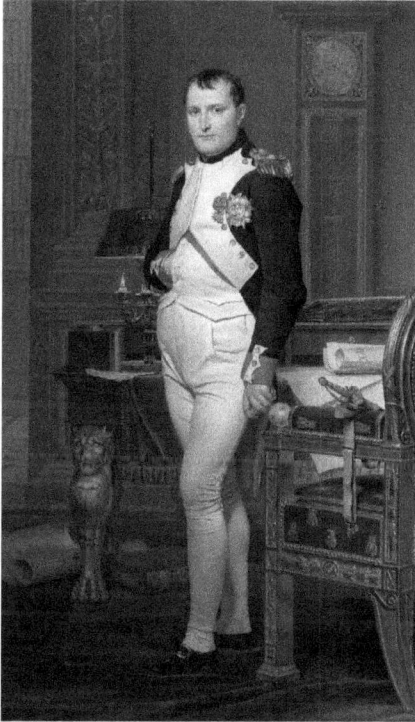

The Emperor Napoleon in His Study at the Tuileries
(1812, oil on canvas)
*Jacques-Louis David (1748-1825) French Neoclassical
painter*

Nothing is more precious

Nothing is more difficult, and therefore more precious, than to be able to decide.
Napoleon Bonaparte *(1769-1821), French military and political leader.*

Permanent decisions and ephemeral decisions

I observed that using words on paper to improve understanding involved recording conclusions about how the world worked, and that these conclusions could be considered a type of permanent decision.

For example, the conclusion that the Earth is round and not flat, or the conclusion that the Earth revolves around the sun, can be considered permanent decisions. These decisions hold until better permanent decisions come along.

However, decisions such as what clothes to wear today, or how to respond to a perceived insult, or which sales pitch to use, can be considered temporary decisions, or ephemeral decisions. These decisions are "throw-away" decisions, and must be made over and over again.

I started using the word "expertise" to refer to the skill of making good ephemeral decisions. I found that when I went back and substituted the term "expertise improvement" for "self-improvement" in my previous insights, the insights were still valid.

Chapter VII

Feedback and Adjustment

Of Ideas and Behavior

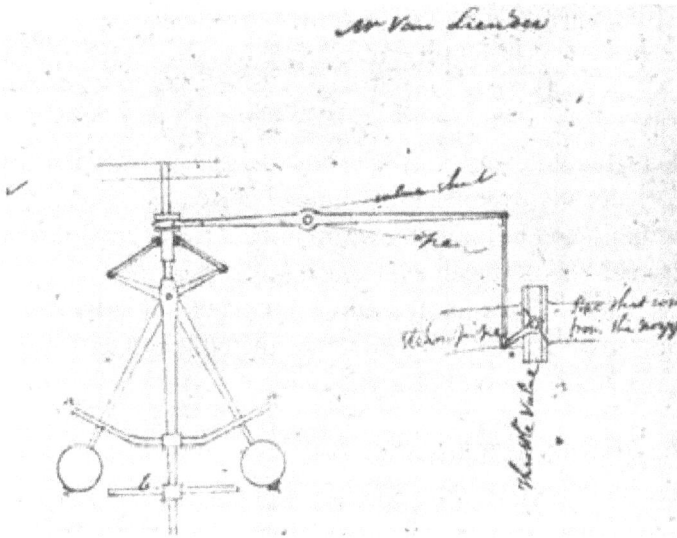

Centrifugal Governor (1798, design sketch)
Matthew Boulton *(1728-1809) English manufacturer,*
James Watt *(1736-1819) Scottish inventor.*

Centrifugal governor

https://en.wikipedia.org/wiki/Centrifugal_governor
(01/18/2016).

In a largely overlooked passage from his famous 1858
paper to the Linnean Society (which led Darwin to publish
On the Origin of Species), British naturalist and explorer
Alfred Russel Wallace (1823-1913) says of the
evolutionary principle:

The action of this principle is exactly like that of the
centrifugal governor of the steam engine, which checks and
corrects any irregularities almost before they become
evident; and in like manner no unbalanced deficiency in the
animal kingdom can ever reach any conspicuous
magnitude, because it would make itself felt at the very
first step, by rendering existence difficult and extinction
almost sure soon to follow.

Adjusting improvement

My engineering education, my software development
experience, and my success with hectosophies all
encouraged me, for many years, to set goals and use trial
and error for all personal learning and improvement.

This worked poorly for people-related improvement. Trial
and error involves a certain amount of failure for each unit
of success. To get more success you must increase your
failure rate. When alone, failure is usually harmless and
can be ignored, but when dealing with others failure has a
cost. When improving interpersonal relationships, you
want to minimize failure while still maximizing
improvement.

In the last half of 2015, for improving interpersonal
relationships, I switched from using trial and error to using

the approach of *adjust toward harmony*. This approach worked better than trial and error.

In early 2016, I again switched, to using the approach of *adjust away from strife*. This worked better yet, but I felt there was still something missing.

A discussion with a good friend helped explain why I was having trouble. We identified the following riddle. Insight followed after the riddle was articulated.

The riddle of friendship betterment

When adjusting a friendship...

- Aiming for a better you is a poor aim; it excludes the friend.
- Aiming for a better friend is a poor aim; you may not adjust friends, only yourself.
- Aiming for a better friendship is a poor aim; it is too vague to be of help when comparing options.

So, if you exclude improving yourself, and exclude improving your friend, and exclude improving the friendship, what is left that can be improved?

Two one-way streets

Friendship is not a two-way street; it comprises two one-way streets. When friendship flows from Celia to you, Celia is a friend *to* you, and you are a friend *of* Celia's. When friendship flows from you to Celia, you are a friend *to* Celia, and Celia is a friend *of* yours.

You are only allowed to improve the friendship flowing *from* you. Thus,

*Be a better friend (**to** your friends).*

In addition, you can (and should) improve the appreciation you show of the friendship flowing *to* you. Thus,

Show more appreciation (of your friends' friendship).

Keeping the concept of adjustment results in

Make steady adjustments to
Be a better friend.
Show more appreciation.

Team adjustment

Team membership is similar to friendship, in that it involves one-way flows. There is a flow of duty from you to the team, a flow of benefits from the team to you, a flow of support from you to other team members, and a flow of support from other team members to you.

Again, improve the flows *from* you, and show appreciation of the flows *to* you.

Make steady adjustments to
Be a better team member.
Give better support to other team members.
Show more appreciation.

Improve the verbs

When dealing with nature, improve the nouns; when dealing with people, improve the verbs.

Walking and adjusting at the same time

If I am walking with two other men, each of them will serve as my teacher. I will pick out the good points of the one and imitate them, and the bad points of the other and correct them in myself.
Confucius *(551-479 BC), Chinese philosopher.*

It's up to you

To you, the person who is irked,
And not to the person who is the jerk,
God assigns the task of fixing
This current condition you find so vexing.
To you, who knows better – that's the clue –
That is why it's up to you.
Easy, you think? You need to be humbler –
Do not assume you can alter the bumbler.
Scold? Or ask? Or teach? – how arrogant!
*Change, **you** must. Learn, **you** must.*
***Improve** toward a settlement.*

Chapter VIII

Accumulism

Six Types of Subjective Learning

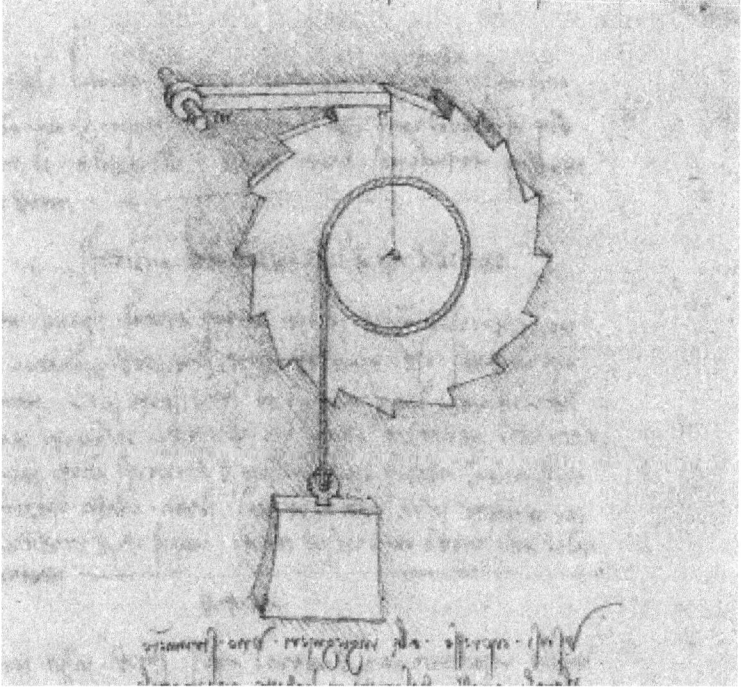

Ratchet and pawl mechanism (manuscript illustration)
Codex Madrid I, page 117r
Leonardo Da Vinci (1452-1519) Italian painter, sculptor, scientist.

Not so simple

There is a quote attributed to the German-born American physicist Albert Einstein (1879-1955) – "Everything should be made as simple as possible, but not simpler".

In the rest of this book, for good or bad, I use quotes without researching their origin to the point of finding page numbers in authored texts. However, with this quote, I tried to find the canonical source. The closest verifiable words of Einstein I could find were from an article Einstein wrote that was published in the journal *Philosophy of Science*, Vol. 1, No. 2 (April 1934).

"It can scarcely be denied that the supreme goal of all theory is to make the irreducible basic elements as simple and as few as possible without having to surrender the adequate representation of a single datum of experience."

Ironically, it appears that those who quoted Einstein followed his advice – they repeated the essence of what he said rather than his exact words.

In the real world, there are hundreds of types of learning, all subtly different. To effectively model learning, however, we must simplify. Einstein's words imply there is a sweet spot – a "Goldilocks" model of subjective learning – that is simple but not too simple.

From 1999 to 2009 I vainly tried to make hectosophies work for all subjective learning (implying there was but one type). From 2009 to 2015 I struggled with two types of subjective learning (the improvement of understanding and self-improvement).

A better model

In late 2015 (I will call it 2016) I found, with relief, that if I expanded my model and defined several types of subjective learning, the empirical insights I had gained over the years made more sense.

2016 hectosophy-based learning approach

I currently define six types of subjective learning:

      U' (U prime) – the improvement of understanding
      E' – the improvement of expertise
      H' – the improvement of habits
      B' – the reduction of personal blocks
      T' – the improvement of team memberships
      F' – the improvement of friendships

The above categorization is philosophical opinion. The formality of notation does not imply a relation to mathematical correctness – it merely makes concepts easier to discuss.

Improvement of understanding (U')

Set a goal of understanding something you do not currently understand. Try many ideas. Record what worked. Occasionally summarize and prioritize what worked into a hectosophy (a set of one hundred ideas) or a decasophy (a set of ten ideas).

This type of subjective learning uses *personal judgment* and *trial and error of ideas*.

Improvement of expertise (E')

Do each task or iteration differently for the rest of your life. Record what worked. Occasionally summarize and prioritize what worked into a hectosophy or a decasophy.

Doing each task or iteration differently allows you to both follow words on paper and not follow words on paper. You follow the plan for the current iteration, but do not follow all of what worked previously.

This type of subjective learning uses *personal judgment* and *trial and error of iterations.*

Improvement of habits (H')

Do each task or iteration differently for the rest of your life. Record what you liked. Occasionally summarize and prioritize what you liked into a hectosophy or a decasophy.

Let your emotions tell you what is better.

This type of subjective learning uses *personal feelings* and *trial and error of iterations.*

Reduction of personal learning blocks (B')

Personal learning blocks arise from an irrational conclusion about the world or about yourself. If you ignore them, they will not go away, and if you struggle against them, they will not go away. It is best to acknowledge them and then learn around or past them, letting them dwindle on their own.

This is a special type of subjective learning that uses *acknowledgement without struggle.*

Improvement of team memberships (T')

Make steady adjustments to be a better team member, give better support, and show more appreciation. Do your assigned job. Be average on the team, and let the team excel.

Record what worked. Occasionally summarize and prioritize what worked into a hectosophy or a decasophy.

This type of subjective learning uses *personal judgment* and *adjustment*.

Improvement of friendships (F')

Make steady adjustments to be a better friend and show more appreciation. Without sacrificing your own happiness, give happiness to others.

Record what you liked. Occasionally summarize and prioritize what you liked into a hectosophy or a decasophy.

Let your emotions tell you what is better.

This type of subjective learning uses *personal feelings* and *adjustment*.

Single axes of learning and improvement (SALI's)

Each of the above types of learning attempts to define a single axis of learning and improvement (SALI) along which to improve. A SALI does not use measurement (metrics). Rather, a SALI is used when subjectively comparing two ideas or actions.

Metrics are more powerful than SALI's, but SALI's are more broadly applicable. SALI's are more powerful than judgment alone, but judgment alone is more broadly applicable.

Trial and error vs. adjustment

I found that trial and error helped single-person improvement, while making steady adjustments helped interpersonal-relationship improvement.

U', E', and H' are forms of single-person improvement; these use trial and error. T' and F' are forms of relationship improvement; these use adjustment.

There are two types of trial and error. U' uses the trial and error of ideas. New ideas are continually tried, and the best ones kept. E' and H' use the concept of doing each iteration differently for the rest of your life, which is a form of trial and error based on time intervals.

Judgment vs. feelings

Understanding, expertise, and team membership (U', E' and T') are not directly affected by what you like or dislike. For these types of improvement, use personal judgment. Observe and record what worked.

Habits and friendship (H' and F') *are* directly affected by what you like or dislike. For these types of improvement, consult your feelings. Reflect on and record what you liked and disliked.

Three types of objective learning

Though not the subject of this book, three types of objective learning are defined to put subjective learning types in context:

      S'   Western science
      M'   Western medical science
      Q'   Metric-based quality improvement

Western science (S')

Before the 1600s, humans learned about nature haphazardly. After the 1600s, humans learned about nature systematically, using what is often called Western science.

Scientific Journal Articles

https://en.wikipedia.org/wiki/Scientific_journal
(01/07/2016).

The publication of the results of research is an essential part of the scientific method. If [scientific journal articles] are describing experiments or calculations, they must supply enough details that an independent researcher could repeat the experiment or calculation to verify the results. Each such journal article becomes part of the permanent scientific record.

The history of scientific journals dates from 1665, when the French Journal Des Sçavans and the English Philosophical Transactions of the Royal Society first began systematically publishing research results. Over a thousand, mostly ephemeral, were founded in the 18th century, and the number has increased rapidly after that.

Western medical science (M')

Before the 1800s, the practice of medicine advanced haphazardly. After the 1800s, the practice of medicine advanced systematically.

Clinical trials

https://en.wikipedia.org/wiki/Clinical_trial (01/23/2016)

Although early medical experimentation was often performed, the use of a control group to provide an accurate comparison for the demonstration of the intervention's efficacy was generally lacking. ... Lind conducted the first systematic clinical trial in 1747. ... After 1750 the discipline began to take its modern shape.

[Refers to Scottish physician James Lind (1716-1794)]

Metric-based quality improvement (Q')

Before the mid-1900s, manufacturing assembly lines were improved haphazardly. After the mid-1900s, manufacturing assembly lines were improved systematically, based on quality improvement techniques developed in Japan.

Measurement, proof, judgment, and emotions

Measurement and proof are objective; judgment and emotions are subjective. Each is important.

Applying a learning philosophy to itself

Life has been evolving for billions of years on Earth. However, life started evolving *fast* during the Cambrian explosion (a little more than 500 million years ago).

While many researchers propose a single reason for this increase in the speed of evolution, perhaps it was a confluence of several reasons.

Any philosophy of learning, continually applied to itself, should theoretically improve, and eventually converge toward the same set of learning techniques – those that "work". This improvement, however, will not be constant.

My learning ideas slowly improved during the past twenty years, but recently they started improving faster.

I think the most important insights that, when combined, contributed to the recent increase in the pace of improvement are:
- The hectosophy – the concept of continually summarizing what worked into a fixed size list.
- The concept of *do each iteration differently for the rest of your life*.

- Defining at least four types of subjective learning (I currently define six).
- Using both judgment and emotions to determine what is "better".
- The concept of adjusting verbs – especially adjusting what flows from you to other people.

Accumulism needs more work

I believe these five insights (combined with lesser insights), when fed back on themselves, will continue to operate as a positive feedback loop. Learning improvements will continue to occur – faster than they have been occurring, but still relatively slowly.

My instincts say two more special insights are needed before an exponential "elbow", or "hockey stick", is reached. I cannot predict what these future insights will look like – I am always surprised when and where insights occur.

Articulating the *words-on-paper learning paradox*, and the *friendship betterment riddle*, was enlightening. Future insights may uncover another subjective-learning paradox, riddle, or catch-22.

We are all as blind men trying to improve the same elephant. Future insights may better integrate accumulism with other theories and practices of learning and personal growth.

Personal learning does not replace education – it adds to it. Future insights may better integrate accumulism with formal teaching and personal coaching.

Future insights may better integrate accumulism with religious wisdom.

A philosophy by any other name

I collectively named my learning insights "accumulism" for convenience. The name is not important. However, I sincerely believe that the study of learning *is* important. It would make me happy to see more classes, and more books, ponder learning as a philosophy.

Verb philosophies

In fact, I would like to generalize my wish. It would make me happy to see more classes, and more books, ponder verb philosophies. By "verb philosophies", I mean philosophical studies of the best way to "do" things.

Learning, teaching, athletic coaching, personal coaching, software development, politics, and economic improvement, among many others, are verbs (or can be made into verbs) that might benefit from exploration by philosophers.

An author's bias

All authors have viewpoints, flaws, and biases. Some authors (for example those of textbooks and biographies) have an obligation to minimize the impact of their biases on their writing.

Authors publishing subjective collections of what worked for them, such as this book, have an obligation to *maximize* the impact of their biases on their writing.

This book contains what worked for me. Astute readers will deduce my viewpoints, flaws, and biases from my writing, and adjust which parts of the book they study, and which parts they ignore.

Existing schools of thought

While I was developing my learning ideas, the words of English statesman and philosopher Francis Bacon (1561-1626) and American software developer and inventor Ward Cunningham (1949-) influenced me most.

After I cobbled my ideas together, I retroactively compared them to existing schools of thought.

1. Within traditional philosophy, accumulism seems to extend Pragmatism – the philosophy of American philosophers Charles Sanders Peirce (1839-1914), William James (1842-1910), and John Dewey (1859-1952). Peirce's description of abductive reasoning seems to describe how ideas of a hectosophy are chosen.

2. The idea of a hectosophy – a finite set of named paragraphs – extends the idea of a pattern language, described by American architect and author Christopher Alexander (1936-) and Ward Cunningham.

3. English philosopher and biologist Herbert Spencer (1820-1903) used the phrase "survival of the fittest" to describe English naturalist and geologist Charles Darwin's (1809-1882) idea of natural selection. Computer scientists use artificial survival-of-the-fittest algorithms. A hectosophy is a survival-of-the-fittest mechanism that culls ideas.

4. The study of human behavior and the improvement of subjective decision making are part of a traditional liberal arts education. A liberal arts education *trains* (as opposed to teaches) students to analyze human behavior and make good subjective decisions by requiring them to analyze and decide hundreds and hundreds of times. Perhaps accumulism is a self-applied liberal arts education.

Abductive reasoning

https://en.wikipedia.org/wiki/Abductive_reasoning
(01/18/2016).

Abductive reasoning (also called abduction, abductive inference or retroduction) is a form of logical inference which goes from an observation to a theory which accounts for the observation, ideally seeking to find the simplest and most likely explanation. In abductive reasoning, unlike in deductive reasoning, the premises do not guarantee the conclusion. One can understand abductive reasoning as "inference to the best explanation".

The fields of law, computer science, and artificial intelligence research renewed interest in the subject of abduction.

A liberal arts education

http://en.wikipedia.org/wiki/Liberal_arts_education
(05/29/2015).

The liberal arts (Latin: *artes liberales*) are those subjects or skills that in classical antiquity were considered essential for a free person (Latin: *liberal*, "worthy of a free person") to know in order to take an active part in civic life, something that (for Ancient Greece) included participating in public debate, defending oneself in court, serving on juries, and most importantly, military service. Grammar, logic, and rhetoric were the core liberal arts, while arithmetic, geometry, the theory of music, and astronomy also played a (somewhat lesser) part in education.

In modern times, *liberal arts education* is a term that … can refer to certain areas of literature, languages, art history, music history, philosophy, history, mathematics, psychology, and science … the term generally refers to matters not relating to the professional, vocational, or technical curricula.

Studying and learning

By *studying* any of several liberal arts, one *learns* two important arts – the art of understanding human behavior, and the art of making good subjective decisions.

Ability to deal with people

Some problems are just too complicated for rational, logical solutions. They admit of insights, not answers.
Jerome B. Wiesner (1915-1994), American scientist, engineer.

Strive not to be a success, but rather to be of value.
Albert Einstein (1879-1955), German-born American physicist.

You can have everything in life that you want if you just give enough other people what they want.
Hilary "Zig" Ziglar (1926-2012), American author, salesman, motivational speaker.

The ability to deal with people is as purchasable a commodity as sugar or coffee and I will pay more for that ability than for any other under the sun.
John D. Rockefeller (1839-1937), American businessman and philanthropist.

Chapter IX

Applied Philosophy

Accumulism in the Real World

Alexander the Great Founding Alexandria
(1737, oil on canvas)
***Placido Costanzi** (1702-1759), Italian painter.*

Through the lens of accumulism

This chapter looks at real world problems.

Software development improvement

If we assume software development is an expertise-based endeavor, the words-on-paper learning paradox applies – to use words-on-paper to improve software development, you must follow the words on paper, and you must not follow the words on paper. Another way to say this is that if you collect best practices, you must not follow them.

The above paragraph is intended to be provocative. Less provocatively, accumulism suggests that software developers choose a different set of practices to follow for each project, and then follow the practices as closely as possible during the project.

At the end of the project, the developers would review the results of using the chosen practices, and for the next project, choose a different set of practices.

For example – two backlogs

This example has no direct link to accumulism. I present it to my software developer friends as an example of a software development practice to try on a project.

Keep two backlogs of unfinished tasks. The customer controls and prioritizes one backlog, while the technical team lead controls and prioritizes the other backlog.

Ninety percent of development time is spent reducing the customer's backlog, and ten percent of development time is spent reducing the team lead's backlog.

Education improvement

If we assume education is an expertise-based endeavor, then, as for software development, the learning paradox applies – you must follow words on paper, and you must not follow words on paper.

In other words, do not converge.

Perhaps a teacher, each semester, could choose a set of practices to follow, and then follow them closely. At the end of the semester, the teacher could review the results of using those practices.

Business improvement

Billions of dollars of worth have been created by using metrics to improve manufacturing to the point that each widget is produced exactly as the previous widget.

Consequently, there is tremendous pressure to attempt to solve other problems as if they were manufacturing problems, by trying to use metrics, and to make iterations identical.

Accumulism suggests, however, that expertise-based endeavors should not be improved this way. To speed learning in an expertise-based endeavor, each iteration of a repeating process should be done *differently*, not *identically*.

The irony of profit and shareholder value

A business should have a good aim for its improvement. This aim should *not* be to maximize profit or shareholder value.

Ironically, *aiming* to maximize profit or shareholder value will not *achieve* maximum profit or shareholder value.

Like a pot of gold at the end of a rainbow, or a squirrel, if you explicitly chase profit you will never catch it. You must let profit come to you.

I am not positive, but I am fairly certain the theoretical improvement goal of a company should be to maximize the ratio of customer happiness divided by production cost. The formula for this would be the following.

Business goal
        = maximize (customer happiness/production cost).
        = maximize (H/C).

If a company can get its (H/C) ratio higher than the (H/C) ratio of its competitors, profit will scurry in the door on its own.

Summary

Britannia between Scylla and Charybdis, or The vessel of
the Constitution steered clear of the Rock of Democracy,
and the Whirlpool of Arbitrary-Power
(1793, engraving, political cartoon)
*James Gillray (1756-1815), British caricaturist and
printmaker.*

To ponder learning as a philosophy is useful.

You need not make your field objective – you can keep your field subjective and still attain systematic improvement.

Solve engineering problems. Navigate social issues.

To improve understanding and know-how:
>Set an ambitious, motivating goal.
>Try many things and record what worked.
>Occasionally summarize what worked in a *hectosophy* or *decasophy*.

To use words on paper for expertise improvement, you must *fully* follow the words on paper, and you must **not** follow the words on paper.

To improve expertise and habits, do each iteration differently for the rest of your life.

Be a better friend. Show more appreciation.

This wonderful world was created such that

>*Individuals who better help others win.*
>*Societies with a better understanding of God win.*

To create worth, help others. To create more worth, join a team that helps others. To retain more worth, own a team that helps others. Maximize the ratio of customer happiness divided by production cost.

A mean team will defeat a same-sized nice team; a nice team will have more members.

Societies with bounded competition advance faster then societies with no bounds (law of the jungle), and societies with no competition (communes). Societies with better-bounded competition (loose but not too loose) win.

Obey the law and worship your God. Learn to learn. Associate with others who do the same.

I love to win,
I love to lose,
The grandest fun
Is to improve.

Ever tried. Ever failed. No matter. Try Again. Fail again. Fail better.
Samuel Beckett *(1906-1989), Irish playwright, novelist.*

I believe that man will not merely endure: he will prevail. He is immortal, not because he alone among creatures has an inexhaustible voice, but because he has a soul, a spirit capable of compassion and sacrifice and endurance.
William Faulkner *(1897-1962), American author.*

Knowledge for the sake of understanding, not merely to prevail, that is the essence of our being. None can define its limits, or set its ultimate boundaries.
Vannevar Bush *(1890-1974), U.S. electrical engineer, physicist.*

Never give in, never give in, never; never; never; never – in nothing, great or small, large or petty – never give in except to convictions of honor and good sense.
Winston Churchill *(1874-1965), British statesman, author.*

The Author

Stan Silver has been developing software for twenty years. He served as a captain in the U.S. Army, and has a master's degree in Aerospace Engineering from M.I.T., with a concentration in feedback control theory.

His curiosity about subjective learning was piqued when, after several years as a software developer, he realized he had no idea how to systematically improve software development.

www.accumulism.com
stan@accumulism.com